Your call is important to us.

Please hold.

John Graham

Hoogstraten, Belgium
2012

John Graham

Your call is important to us. Please hold.

© 2012 John Graham

Published by **The Copper Beech,**
ETCetera Assessments LLP,
Deken Sendenstraat 13
Hoogstraten, Belgium 2320

ISBN: 1468098802

EAN-13: 9781468 098808

Printed and bound in the United States of America.
The text is formatted in Times New Roman, while its
Titles, header and footer are in Bradley Hand ITC TT.

For information on translations or distribution of this
book please contact the author at author@webetc.info

Your call is important to us.

Please hold.

John Graham

"Your call is important to us.
Please stay on the line until your call
is no longer important to you."

With acknowledgements to Mike Baldwin

Foreword

"Your call is important to us. Please hold."

We wince at the plea to join the long line of callers on hold. We grit our teeth knowing full well that our call is no more important than anyone else's, yet sometimes there is no alternative but to 'hold' since there is no other way to make contact.

Governments often go one better: they offer a user-friendly menu of possibilities from which you may choose. Some of the possibilities lead back in circles to a junction through which you have already passed, and some offer the promise of a response: "We are experiencing an unusually large number of calls at this time. Your call will be answered in the order it was received. Please hold. Your call is important to us." Other options end with a "Good-bye."

These standard phone brush-offs seem more personable than the e-mail address, which usually drops your message or query into a black bottomless pit and only occasionally elicits a 'do-not-reply' acknowledgement that your e-mail was received. Neither is personable. Both are symptomatic of the general malaise of organization, either public or private, that no one cares.

We tend to think of national and local government as being the only offenders in this respect but companies also breed their own types of response that exhibit the same brand of sickness. It is worth taking note and demanding action wherever one can.

This book goes a little beyond trying to get someone to answer a question; this book opposes over-government and poor communication, especially in its contact with clients, by demonstrating the failings, some merely ridiculous and some extremely dangerous.

It is difficult to speak of those clerks without referring also to the regulations and rules behind them, with which they have to comply and, sometimes, explain. Often the rules are so uncompromising, nonsensical, damaging, obstructive and/or just plain foolish that it takes a very special person to act as their spokesperson. That 'special' person must either have not given their job much thought, beyond its pay-slip, or must have not known enough to see that a rule may be actually damaging to the person before them. Otherwise they would seek a more meaningful job or do a better job by suggesting alternative ways. Thus, the actions of the clerk say many things about that person him or herself.

Recently, a Texas communicator for a welfare office said, "Even though it (an application for aide) was processed according to our procedures, it does not comfort them at all."(!) It certainly didn't comfort the poor woman in question who was seeking aide for her hungry and barefoot children. After having gone through procedures four times to meet refusal four times, she shot herself and her children in the badly named 'Human Services and Welfare' office.

The worst kind of dictatorship is the benign unapproachable variety apparently ruled by plebeian clerks. There is in Texas a clerk who believes that using procedures should bring you 'comfort.' Sometimes those plebeian clerks, as you will see, worm their way up to real destructive power.

I hope that at times the book brings tears of laughter to your eyes and at other times, just tears.

If you are a government or company representative, or someone who has responsibility for public communications and for dealing with the public, then these tales may give you food for thought.

If your are a government or company employee with some responsibility for decision making, then this book may also encourage you to think how your decisions may affect others outside your immediate department. Procedures are there to help your clerks do their jobs not to 'comfort' an applicant on the edge of despair.

The book is based primarily on almost 80 years of experience with residence in five countries in two continents together with a wealth of travel across the globe. It also benefits from the opinions of good friends who extend my experience with their own in different parts of the world.

I am grateful to Colin Bazell in the United Kingdom, to Donald Haines in the Netherlands, to Mieke Roos in Belgium and to Michael Buehner-Coldrey in the United States for their advice and experience in dealing with government. Mieke Roos selected the title.

The book is based on real experience, wide research and a little communication theory. The final chapters draw conclusions from these generally sad tales. The book also provides examples of how to deal with civil servants: often very successful methods worthy of your consideration.

At best, even though it is needed by any society, government and the 'assistance' it offers is worth great skepticism.

John Graham

This book is dedicated to all those who have suffered from the arrogance of civil servants and their equivalent in private business and, so it is especially dedicated to Mieke Roos who has just survived a year in which she managed the building of a new house and home.

Contents

Foreword 5

Introduction 11

A Society's Origins 20

Creating Governance 31

Financial Management 39

Security – managing protection 48

Times past and times abroad 53

Mandating what is good for you 67

The dangers 80

Adoption 87

Importing a car 121

Managing payment 138

Understanding 144

What makes a bad civil servant? 150

What makes a good civil servant? 163

With the shoe on the other foot 173

The Fuzzy bit 177

In summary 183

Bibliography 187

John Graham

Notes: 189

Introduction

Any society needs governance for it to operate.

Traditionally, throughout the ages, strong men have ruled and unilaterally determined what was good for their society. They held power by force of arms and yet made some allowance for the minions who they supported and whom they needed. That allowance was not much: a serf was not allowed to do much more than serve his or her master, and he was expected to be compliant. The strong man, whether he was Attila the Hun, Pope Leo X, Tsar Ivan the Terrible, or Muammar al-Gaddafi, provided the governance of his society as he thought fit.[1] His 'civil servants' or 'communicators' relayed his governance to his people, even though the civil servants may have gone by different titles before the twentieth century.

King Herod created a kingdom for Rome from taxes levied upon those who resided in Judea (after payments to Rome of course). Joseph, a carpenter and a taxpayer, met Herod's civil servants, who were then called tax collectors, in Jerusalem and he suffered from their rigid adherence to rules. For example, his whole family had to appear before them including his pregnant wife who had to endure an arduous journey for no good reason other than by the government's rules she had to be shown to exist. These tax collectors were also census takers.

It is worth noting that beyond the tax collectors in Jerusalem, Joseph must have been notified of the need

---

[1] As you will see, you could also add Sam Walton of Wal-Mart to this list.

to attend to them by other civil servants of the state: 'criers' who went through the alleys of Bethlehem calling out the regulations: that is that he should travel to Jerusalem.

The Chinese established the first civil service of qualified officials responsible for regulating society according to the emperor's edicts.[2] The scrolls on which the regulations were written were bound with red tape. A civil servant would be then responsible for one or more regulations but nothing could happen until they could get through the red tape. Modern society has inherited the red tape and the taxes and rules that it binds. 'Red tape' obscures and delays interactions with institutions.

But there have been free thinkers throughout history who wanted more than merely the opportunity to pay taxes or to work as serfs: they wanted 'choice.' In medieval Europe a new class of freemen arose. They were those who made more than they could sell locally, so they travelled and traded on their own behalf in other towns. Because it was not known to what city it was to which they owed allegiance, they became 'freemen'. However, even then they came under the governance of the local bishop or emperor where they principally lived and occasionally that yoke irked. They often revolted for 'freedom' but even success of a revolution didn't result in much more than a change of yokes in the 14th Century.

The Russian revolution of 1917 threw off dictatorship and showed what a central free Soviet government could do. In a direct reversal of the Tsarist class

---

[2] Han Dynasty (206 BC to AD 220)

system, personal position and property was ruled to be secondary to the common good. At the same time, personal initiative and ambition had no place in a society in which everyone was judged to be equal. To bring this about, the revolutionaries established a government of local committees at every level, even to individual apartments,[3] to ensure that everyone worked and that no one got more than they deserved. They were the ultimate 'civil servants.'

In 1945, George Orwell, satirically demonstrated[4] that while everyone was judged to be equal in Soviet society, some were more equal than others ... especially when they were part of the governing class, for even while no class differences were said to exist, the civil servants ruled.

Joseph Vissarionovich Djugashvili, Stalin, was a government servant who became Commissar of the Workers and Peasant's Inspectorate. He scrambled his way up from there. He was a civil servant. However, at the height of his power he was no less a tyrant than the Tsars that he had replaced. His government, with all its rules and regulations, was even more repressive. He empowered those who administered his rules and they, in turn, with regulations as their weapons, ruled the working class. The penalties for not obeying the rules and regulations could be, and were often, imprisonment, exile or death.

---

[3] *"Dr. Zhivago,"* Boris Pasternak, 1957

[4] *"The Animal Farm,"* George Orwell, 1945

It wasn't that government itself that was an error since 'government' is a necessity for any society. In the Soviet example however repression was exercised by the servants of the government in a mindless and often vicious application of rules.

Even the hippies of San Francisco's Haight-Ashbury district in 1967 needed 'government'. Artist Michael Bowen organized the first Summer-of-Love event. When the 30,000 who attended needed someone to point to a vacant space in which they might crash or to direct them to where they might find counter-cultural psychedelic enlightenment, that 'someone' was a civil servant of sorts. Some of these organizational servants arranged anti-war demonstrations or created groups and communities with very different ideas about the education of children and families. No organization, even in that disorganized period, came about without someone taking charge ... 'local government' grew even among people who declared themselves outside normal society and its government operations.

In 2011, the informal 'Occupy Wall Street' financial opposition movement in New York, which spread to 900 cities world wide[5], was able to establish a web site, a bank account and to collect $300,000 in contributions. In an informal nod to democracy at a local level they even met to agree the purchase of cleaning materials for their park site though they were eventually ejected for the filthy conditions under which they lived.

---

[5] Local Action with Global Message, The Guardian Weekly, 21-27 October 2011, p 1

For example, Nicole Carty, who worked for a television station, spent her free time in Zuccotti Park, 'Occupy Wall Street's' headquarters, organizing general assembly meetings for the demonstrators.[6] She was part of the group's self-appointed governance organization.

In London, a similar informal group was able to set up campsites in various parts of the city and a consensus refused to evacuate the forecourt of St. Paul's Cathedral. An earlier Spanish group (the 'Indignants' movement) took a group decision to go to the European Union headquarters in Brussels and they did make the trip.

Such group actions cannot be accomplished without some sort of organization. Thus, even the informal protest movements of 2011 put together forms of governance in different countries and they used effective organizational volunteer 'civil servants' – clerks.

In today's formal societies, layers of government abound in tiers and in parallel, as all the functions of a society are addressed and even more are invented, for the 'good' of society. In some countries a very large percentage of the population works for some level of government in positions from which they cannot be fired for mere inefficiency. That has been the cause of the economic downfall of many nations, from Greece to Portugal to Ireland to Spain and Italy in the 21st Century.

---

[6] ABC News, "'It Gets Heated': Twin Sisters Divided Over Occupy Wall Street," by Enjoli Francis, October 28, 2011

John Graham

We can all die from the good others wish upon us especially when too many leeches occupy positions of power.

A note on terminology

In this book, the term 'civil servant' is used to denote any member of the government other than those in the military, as in 'civilian'. They are either of high enough rank to be appointed by the politicians in power or, more often, are the plebeian clerks that we meet in offices open to the public.

The term 'civil service' does not mean in this book, as it once did in China and in Britain, a branch of governmental service in which individuals are employed on the basis of professional merit judged by competitive examinations. In the Roman Empire and in China in 850 AD qualified civil servants did the work of government and these were selected either by patronage (in the Roman Empire) or, in early China, by strenuous examinations.[7]

In China:

"The older scholar-officials had pursued learning for its own sake but the new officials under Song Taizong

---

[7] From the time of the Han Dynasty (206 BC to AD 220) until the implementation of the imperial examination system, most appointments in the imperial bureaucracy were based on recommendations from prominent aristocrats and local officials whilst recommended individuals were predominantly of aristocratic rank. Emperor Wu of Han started an early form of the imperial examinations, transitioning from inheritance and patronage to merit, in which local officials would select candidates to take part in an examination of the Confucian classics. (Wikipedia)

were more concerned with figuring out what the Emperor wanted to hear. They became government officials because they had mastered a certain amount of knowledge and were able to parrot it back on a test to the Emperor's satisfaction. They were well educated within very specific parameters and were loyal to the Emperor.[8]

These words, describing officials in 800 – 900 A.D. are remarkably accurate in describing the same officials in Western Europe in 2011 A.D. Nothing apparently changes in the civil service.

Of course, despite the changes to national boundaries, despite more than one hundred wars throughout the globe in each century since 900 AD, one thing above all has not changed: Red Tape bureaucracy. It is alive and well, throughout the world, even in China in 2011.

For example, to obtain a certificate for tax payment on a rental property it requires attendance at the correct tax bureau together with:

- o "ID card copy of property owner. (If property is co-owned, need copies of all owners)"
- o "Rental contract copy. (If the lesee is company, then the company chop is required in contract)"
- o "Original property deed / title documents"
- o "If person going to tax bureau is not owner, then a copy of the person's ID or passport is required plus an authorization letter signed by owner"

---

[8] "*The History of the Medieval World*", Susan Wise Bauer, W.W. Norton, 2010 p. 570

John Graham

- o "A filled-in application form. In Beijing this is the 北京市地方税务局代开发票申请表"

The whole affair could strike terror in the heart of a foreign resident since the requirements are, in Chinese, as follows:

代开发票须知:
一、出租房屋完税并代开发票的相关要求及所需资料:(房屋所在地须为东城区)
　　1、出租人有效身份证明复印件。(共有产权的,提供全部产权人的身份证明复印件)
　　2、房屋租赁协议复印件。(承租方为单位的需要加盖单位公章)
　　3、房产证明原件。(无法提供房产证明原件的,可持2009年4月1日以后由第五税务所开具的完税证原件和发票记账联原件办理)
　　4、非出租人本人办理的,还须提供经办人有效身份证明复印件。
　　5、《授权委托书》复印件。
二、提供劳务完税并代开发票的相关要求及所需资料:(劳务提供者居住地须为东城区)
　　1、提供劳务方的有效身份证明复印件。
　　2、劳务合同复印件。(劳资双方签字,单位须加盖公章)
　　3、非劳务提供方本人办理的,还须提供经办人有效身份证明复印件。
　　4、《授权委托书》复印件。
三、出租个人车辆完税并并代开发票的相关要求及所需资料:
　　1、车主有效身份证明复印件。
　　2、车辆行驶证明复印件。
　　3、车辆租赁协议复印件。(要求租赁双方签字,租赁方为单位的需要加盖单位公章)
　　4、非车主本人办理的,还还须提供经办人有效身份证明复印件。
　　5、《授权委托书》复印件。
注意事项:
　　1、新版身份证要求复印正反两面。
　　2、每月最后一个工作日下午为结账时间,暂停开具完税证及代开发票业务。

While this information is offered half-humorously, I can attest, having lived and bought property in three different countries, to the fact that legal requirements in foreign countries often look as intelligible as this list when half explained by the average civil servant.

In the Roman and Chinese civilizations, senior civil servants and inspectors often met with members of the populace themselves but in the modern world intermediate clerks are employed to deal with the hoi polio. These intermediate clerks are also 'qualified' by being instructed in a very small part of government.

---

9 "*Housing Rental Fapiao*", <http://www.chinaredtape.com/>

It is this set of clerks that we are mostly concerned with in this text, remembering that they are educated within even more confined parameters than their superior.

In this book the term 'civil servant' does not indicate civility; often, as you will see, it is quite the opposite.

Furthermore, as we see, those who deal with the public are often civil servants, or government servants or company servants or even servants of organizations. They might even be volunteers. They are any person who deals with a 'customer', a member of the public, and in that sense they are 'servants' of the public rather than of their employer. Problems arise when they consider themselves to be no servant at all.

John Graham

A Society's Origins

As shown, a society of people living together needs some sort of 'government' once it has become a unit. Let's consider how some societies evolved and what their governance came to be. They were not always ideal.

Belgium

Belgium is a very good recent example of how a society and its governance might evolve.

Belgium became a nation in 1830 when the Low Countries finally, after a very short war that ended centuries of friction, broke apart on grounds of religion. The northern areas of the Low Countries, which had become Protestant following the Lutheran Reformation in 1517, became The Netherlands, while the southern area, all Catholic, became Belgium.

This southern Catholic region, Belgium, was split between the Walloons, who had originally traveled north from Roman Gaul, and the Flemish of Flanders and Brabant, who were mainly Celtic tribes. The Walloons originally spoke Walloon, a dialect of French, but today more coherently speak mainline French.[10] The Flemish spoke a dialect of the northern Dutch. A small eastern German-speaking area was annexed by Belgium in 1920 as part of the reparations for World War I, and it moved backwards and

---

[10] The Walloons might well be descendants of a Visigoth war leader Wallia who, in 417, obtained Roman concurrence to his people settling in Gaul. "The History of the Medieval World," Susan Wise Bauer, Norton, 2010, p. 93

forwards in World War II, but the area plays a very small part in Belgian society or its government.

A royal family rules the entire multi-lingual area. Leopold I, the first king of Belgium was born in Coburg, Bavaria, but he became a British citizen and married into the British royal family. His wife was Princess Charlotte of Wales and he became a close advisor of his niece, Queen Elizabeth of England. He even arranged her marriage.[11] Thus, he and his ensuing family had no inherent connection with either the native Flemish or the native Walloons or the Catholic religion of Belgium as a whole. This is a distinct advantage for his descendant, the present king, who rules a country composed principally of two disruptive and non-cooperative selfish 'children'.

A present point of contention is that Wallonia was originally rich as a result of its coal and steel making, but with the decline of those industries the province became less affluent than its hitherto poorer neighbor, Belgian Flanders. Now many of the Flemish people, remembering their second-grade past, want to exact revenge by casting off their now poorer French sibling to create an independent Flanders. Meanwhile, the Wallonia inhabitants struggle to remain French. English is, from 2012, a formal 'second' school language in Flanders equal to French, thus adding to the decline of French.

Add to this olio the fact that the capital of Belgium, Brussels, is also the principal 'capital' of the European Community with English as its present informal

---

[11] Wikipedia, Leopold I of Belgium,
http://en.wikipedia.org/wiki/Leopold_I_of_Belgium

practical working tongue, which will become a formal requirement in 2015. The Brussels region is literally part of Flanders but in fact has little connection, since in addition to English more French is spoken than Dutch.

This mixture of regions and past and present imperatives forms the background upon which the nation's governance has evolved since 1830 and within which all manner of civil servants spend their waking hours. About 15% of the working population of Belgium work for its governments.

During these years of development, there was never a clear playing field on which to establish an ideal government from scratch. The rules come from history, from political bias, from the fact that some regions were richer than others, and from the reality that a lot of people have to reside in a comparatively small space. There is very little that could be ascribed to 'a square-1' development of a really efficient service to meet the needs of the people.

Thus now, there is a European government, a federal Belgian government, a Flemish government, a Walloon government and a German government, each with a self-appointed responsibility of providing some service to their inhabitants. In reality, these diverse factions are lead by uncooperative small self-serving politicians. Despite unifying royal leadership these factions serve their own purposes and there is enormous duplication of every function of national government as each faction tries to show that they are in charge.

There is almost no cooperation between the political parties. Indeed in 2010 – 2011, the nation had nothing but a caretaker government and a very frustrated king who employed a *'formateur'* to try to establish a consensus government. That position continued until the end of 2011[12] when a new government was formed at the urging of the European Union and the fact that the financial community had noticed that Belgium is not a good risk. The borrowing rate against payments escalated and the Standard and Poor's rating dropped.

It's worth noting that the external International financial community exerts power today on the policies and government of a country. If only it did something for the qualities of the civil servants.

In the meantime, Belgium has established a world record for being a country without a government and its global financial position has steadily worsened.

All this time, the various factions have been fighting for civil rights … recognition, funding, representation. It is doubtful that 'service to the public' has ever entered their deliberations. The Flemish, the Walloons, the Greens, the far right, the far left and the socialists all want what they perceive to be consistent with their own political agenda. And what of the public? "Oh, they'll benefit from what we decide," is clearly what the politicians believe.

Of course, having no leadership does not mean that anarchy exists; regulations are still administered, government or no government. The civil service is self-perpetuating.

All the different national and sub-national and local organizations hire clerks to administer their rules.

---

[12] December 5th 2011

Often the rules differ between locations that are only a few miles apart and, even within the same department, they rarely talk to each other. However, one thing remains the same: the same type of people administers the rules. In general, they lack initiative, ambition, or ability to do more than know the bare essentials of the particular parcel of rules under their care.

Having so many divisions in one nation's civil service provides an additional weapon in any civil servant's armory. If one is French, blame clearly belongs to the Flemish and vice versa. They can simply not do anything if a matter is not purely within their own territory … it's a standard excuse.

Even though we use Belgium as an example, similar arrangements have to be made in all break-ups and alliances of nations or societies.

The United States of America

By contrast the government of the United States is still evolving.

Taking Colorado as an example of the west: towards the end of the 19th Century the only inhabitants were tribal Indians, principally Utes, who lived under tribal earth rules, together with a few settlers. These settlers lived under very basic U.S. rules set forth by a Federal government established 2,000 miles away in the East. These few rules had mainly to do with what a settler might take from the land in terms of property or minerals. The settler was offered in return some occasional military protection from marauding Indians. Much later, law and order and the railway came to protect settlers, principally from themselves. Never was a settler much beholden to a central government and, giving nothing, he received nothing. He learned to administer according to his own needs since he had no history to encumber him.

Now of course, 160 years later, the Federal and State Governments and local governments at the city and minor borough levels, govern society. Fortunately, although there is competition for responsibility there is little duplication. The rules and regulations are far less prohibitive than in older socialist Europe. Original western government still largely applies: in principle a man makes his own way.

Although many parties exist in the United States only two (sometimes three) have a chance of assuming leadership. The civil service is independent of which party assumes power except at the very top.

On one occasion I was party to the hosting of senior civil servant appointees of one political party when the other party was due to take over control. This would mean that individuals who were more compliant to the views of the new ruling political party would replace the prior senior civil servants, and their immediate cadre. The gathered civil servants were thus out looking for a position before they were actually terminated. However, in speaking to them it was clear they didn't mind which political party they worked for. They could easily change their views for a secure position. They demonstrated that the civil service was really independent of politics and what mattered were their own positions.

Britain

In England, the absolute power of kings was somewhat modified in 1215 by the Magna Carta, which made the King answerable to a council of Barons, and a subset of that council, that evolved much later into a

Parliament including the House of Lords and the House of Commons.[13]

Originally, there was no seat of English government (or government offices) since the king conducted his business as he traveled around the country from Gloucester, to Northampton, to Salisbury, to Cambridge, to Winchester and to Shrewsbury.[14] However, from 1337, Edward III increasingly situated his civil service in one place: Westminster Palace in London. His chancellor, treasurer, and other offices of state all issued their letters from permanent offices there from that date onwards.

However, governance of the people in medieval times was still the right of local feudal lords. They set the rules by which serfs worked, contributed to the pantry of the lord and paid taxes when required. Only when the King needed to assemble an army did much change. However, unlike later in the Americas, the church was strong in the British Isles (and in Europe as a whole) so in addition to the local landlord, the local bishopric also governed its flock. Thus, there were dual levels of governance that never existed in the American colonies.

A big difference between Europe and the United States is that the first, in many respects, follows the Soviet pattern. Your residence in Europe must be registered with the authorities and many other rules, taxes, and restrictions follow directly from this. One is essentially

---

[13] "The Story of England," Christopher Hibbert, Phaidon Press Ltd, London, 1992

[14] "The Time Traveler's Guide to Medieval England, Ian Mortimer, Simon and Schuster, 2011 p.17

tied to a town and its administration just as medieval serfs were tied to their counts. By contrast, in the United States, there is no need to register a residence with the authorities unless you want to own property or drive a car or vote. Even the driving license is a minimal tie since you might have a second or third address in other states.

India

A Chinese monk, Faxian, toured India in about 500 AD.[15] He traveled through the lands of Chandragupta, which encompassed about three-quarters of modern Indian continent. Chandragupta ruled with a very light hand.

The people are numerous and happy: they do not have to register their households or attend to any magistrates and their rules. Only those who cultivate the royal land have to pay a portion of the grain from it (are taxed). The king governs without decapitation or other corporal punishment. Criminals are simply fined, lightly or heavily, according to the circumstances (of each case.)

Faxian was impressed with a government that did not need many restrictive rules and officials as he was used being bound by Chinese red tape, just as a European in the 21st century may view United States compared to Europe.

Chandragupta's territories were composed of a central core of his own lands and lands acquired through marriage, surrounded by many independent territories

---

[15] *"The History of the Medieval World,"* Susan Wise Bauer, W.W. Norton, New York, p 26

ruled by kings from whom he only expected tribute. He left these surrounding territories alone and carried over the effective *laissez-faire* government to his own central core of lands. Still he needed a few officials to collect the tributes, the produce of his lands and to provide security.

Thus, all societies are governed according to a number of different origins and while general assumptions can be drawn, each governance system must finally be judged on its own individual merits (and demerits).

Unfortunately, there is commonality among the employees at the lowest levels, whom we call 'civil servants', in all these very different governances. They are the individuals, which the public sees as the first line of the government. They often have the same work and the same personal characteristics whether they administer garbage laws in Belgium, social services in the USA, the military in Britain or sales outlets in India.

This book discusses this interface with the public.

The number of civil servants

Not all government employees meet the public or deal with the public by phone, e-mail or letter, but those who do are probably proportional to the total number of individuals employed by the government.

Comparative statistics are difficult to come by since every country counts differently. Some count all employees in the public sector; some count civil servants within that total, while some count only senior civil servants. However, the number of civil servants amounts to millions in each country. In Canada, for example, 3.6 million are in the civil service, amounting to 21.2% of all jobs. There are so many people to administer the rules that one wonders who does the work.

Europe[16], for example employs large numbers of its population in government service: 0.84 million in Belgium (out of 4.52 million employed persons[17] which means that over 18.6% of the Belgians who are employed, work for the civil service). Numbers are even larger elsewhere: 9% of the total population in Poland, 8% in France, 10% in Latvia and 11% in Sweden. By contrast the U.S.A.[18] employs only about 6.3% of its population in government service. This is a little misleading since many of its functions are administered privately and these private firms also have clerical staff that interacts with the public.

There is one enormous difference between the clerical staff of a company and the civil servants of a government agency. The former can be summarily dismissed for inefficiency or wrongdoing. The latter can almost never be dismissed. This makes a difference that works in favor of the public in the United States and that's why the U.S. is so different from Europe even though the number of people who deal with the public is not so different.

Indeed, no member of the public is immune from having to deal with clerical staff. But members of the

---

[16] Administration and the Civil Service in the EU 27 Member States, MINISTÈRE DU BUDGET, DES COMPTES PUBLICS ET DE LA FONCTION PUBLIQUE, 2008

[17] http://www.tradingeconomics.com/belgium

[18] U.S. Census Bureau 2009

John Graham

clerical staff who do not have a fear of losing their job
react differently to the public from those who could be
out on the street.

Creating Governance

In what follows it is worth remembering that young people emerge into adulthood, or in these days, graduate from college, with two fundamentally different approaches to their coming career. At the most basic levels, some are creative and some are cautious.

Those who are creative will join forward-moving companies with initiative or they will form such companies themselves. They think of the way forward rather than of restrictions or problems that they might encounter.

Those who are cautious will join conservative organizations targeting security or the regulation of 'safety.' They will nearly always view forward-moving companies as being in need of care and restriction. These are the regulators who don't see regulation as a task so much as a semi-religious calling.

Remember this as the text continues.

How do we create governance?

'Need' is what should drive governance.

This sounds so simple.

A farming family needs to build a barn but cannot do it alone, so some good person who knows of other capable people assembles a group one day to build the barn. They do so and everyone enjoys the camaraderie and the family provides some refreshments. Now however, a barn-building function exists and rules begin to appear: who merits a new barn; how is it to be paid for; what designs are permissible; what refreshments should be offered to the volunteers and so forth. Those rules represent 'governance' and the regulation of the work of building a barn. The persons who set the rules and see that they are met are 'civil servants'. Soon they will appoint a person in charge of barn building ... a 'senior civil servant'. At least, in this example, he would probably know what it takes to build a barn.

It is not always so simple.

The Canadian GST

In Canada in 1991 under Premier Mulroney, the federal government needed money. So seeing the profits that Australia and New Zealand reaped from a Value Added Tax (VAT) they decided that was the way to go. It wasn't a done deal until Mulroney appointed an increased number of senators to ensure passage of the Canadian Goods and Services Tax (GST) bill.[19]

Moreover, rather than first 'building a barn' to test the idea, the Canadian government appointed a Minister in charge of the GST. Since Canada didn't have a VAT or a GST, the Minister knew nothing of its consequences other than what he might have seen on a paid trip to the Antipodes. He viewed himself merely as the super tax collector. So, he first decided the number of people required to collect the new tax

---

[19] Michelle Salvail, The Goods and Services Tax: The Government's Administrative Costs, The Government of Canada, 1994, http://dsp-psd.pwgsc.gc.ca/CollectionR/LoPBdP/BP/bp377e.htm#A._Startup_Costs(txt)

across the various provinces of Canada, the rules by which they should operate, and the need for a new Ministry building to house his staff. Naturally the building had to compete with the grandeur of other Ministry buildings. He hired the staff, issued the new regulations and moved into the new marble Ministry building. By these actions, he spent $820 million, and thereby guaranteed that the new tax would provide no income to the government for several years until the infrastructure that he had set in place was paid for.

Fortunately, the collection of GST and the payments for a new Ministry building appear in different financial ledgers, so the Minister was safe. GST income could not be penalized by the cost of the civil service organization producing it. Taking care not to be held accountable is a working principle at many levels of the civil service, from top to bottom.

In this Canadian example, with a very compliant electorate, need was supplanted by government fiat.[20] Only finances were considered ... such things as increased paperwork, increased accounting at all levels of manufacture, and increased hiring to take care of the increased work were not considered as burdens on the population.

Belgian Recycling

Need is also often supplanted by political grandstanding. A senior civil servant often goes beyond his mandate by forcing unneeded 'services' on the population. In this way he makes his name known.

---

[20] Presently the GST is 5% but it is compounded with a Harmonized Sales Tax (HST) of 13%. This compares with European VATs, which range up to 23%.

In some places, presently, a vigorous 'green' program drives the collection and recycling of garbage. Various reasons are given, including the finite limit of resources, the finite limit of garbage-disposal sites, the need to protect the environment, global warming, and the provision of additional income to the local administration, which is advertised as 'lightening the citizen's tax burden'.

In the north of Belgium, in Hoogstraten, all these arguments are used as if they were national imperatives. They are not. In fact neither the city of Brussels nor the city of Antwerp (totaling 15% of the Belgian population) recycle garbage for any of those advertised imperatives. The recycling of garbage is neither cost effective nor is it needed.

So? Is this a social service? Does it fulfill a need?

The collection of waste for the society certainly is a social service and it merits appropriate payment. Assistance for **voluntary** waste segregation would also be a social service. However, the **demand** that waste be segregated is not a service but merely a political imposition, since it does not assist anyone but the grandstanding politician.

Furthermore, those that administer such a service according to rules rapidly become more accustomed to the rules than to any idea of service. The concept that they are servants of the community is quickly lost as they assume the role of judge and jury in collecting garbage according to their interpretation of the rules.

For example, if a can of waste does not conform to the rules of what might be contained, it is rejected in its entirety with a curt notice of default. The idea that the rubbish collector should collect the waste and perhaps, at most, separate out the offending item seems to evade them.

The idea that these servants are appointed to help society is no longer apropos for 'a service' that becomes an end in its own right.

Large debris in this same town must be personally transported to a 'container park'. There the incoming vehicle (usually a car and a trailer) is weighed and the charge is reckoned on the reduction of weight after waste has been left. The deliverer must dispose of the waste personally. This involves unloading the waste by hand and carrying each piece individually up 8 to 10 steps to drop it into a container. The idea of allowing a load of waste to be tipped from your trailer into a container below the vehicle's level is not considered. That would be a service to the taxpayer.

Prohibition in the USA

In January 1919, the United States Congress ratified an amendment to the U.S. Constitution.[21] The 18th amendment prohibited the manufacture, transportation and sale of alcoholic drinks and in 1920 it went into effect. It had been proposed and pushed into legislation by an odd alliance of pressure groups ranging from those who wanted no alcohol of any kind in any product drinkable or not, to those who objected to brewers with a German background (Pabst, Coors, Budweiser and Schlitz), to those in favor of women's suffrage, and to those who wanted to repeal prior anti-racist legislation.

---

[21] "Last Call ... the Rise and Fall of Prohibition," Daniel Okrent, Scribner, 2011

The Volstead Act of 1919 that set out the regulations for the amendment, followed. It created governance. Its 67 sections encompassed everything from definitions and exceptions, to boundaries of operation such as how close a foreign ship carrying liquor could approach U.S. territory, to the organization of the amendment and finally to penalties incurred by its violation.

The Volstead Act also created a need for 4,000 agents and 4,000 clerical staff, all of whom were government servants.

This organization was no service to the general population, it was a service to the 'dry' pressure group, which wanted the prohibition of alcohol, and so it remained until the amendment was repealed in 1929.

Greek Civil Obesity

Some nations keep the rate of unemployment low by excessive hiring into governance jobs. Unfortunately, they often bankrupt the state by the resulting excessive expenditure.

In 2010 it was apparent that Greece was insolvent. The nation had been spending far beyond its means and its apparent prosperity encouraged investors. When the bottom dropped out the investors left and Greece had to be bailed out by billions of dollars in loans from the European Union (EU) and Germany in particular.

In order that those loans be safeguarded the EU forced Greek to undertake some austerity. It is not at all certain that the loans might not be outright losses anyway especially as the Greeks who supported all the spending don't like being told they must now save instead. They showed this dislike in mindless riots.

Part of Greek spending was the obesity of its civil governance so austerity meant cutting the civil service. Planned measures included the following:

- A new (read 'lesser') pay and promotion system covering all 700,000 civil servants,
- Further cuts in public sector wages and many bonuses scrapped,
- Some 30,000 public sector workers suspended, wages would be cut to 60% and they would face lay-off after one year,
- Wage bargaining would be suspended,
- Monthly pensions above 1,000€ would be cut 20% above that level,
- There were other cuts in pensions and lump-sum retirement pay,
- And the Tax-free threshold would be lowered to 5,000€ a year from 8,000€.

So it was apparent that Greece had hired 700,000 public service workers and then overpaid them. This was for a population of 11.31 million. Each Greek government worker 'served' just 15 other Greeks. This is real governance obesity. No wonder that the holders of these well-paid sinecures objected to having their benefits cut.

In the United States

In the United States cuts are being made in many cities as a result of the 2010 recession. For example, Chicago is steadily cutting its public service workers and proudly announces that at the end of 2011 it will employ 32,300 civil servants, a 23% drop since 2002.[22] However, this simply points to the fact that the city was fat, dumb and happy in prior years paying thousands of unresponsive civil servants beyond the city's needs.

Thus, while governance and the civil service are necessary for any society, they can be overdone especially as, you will see, the service is generally not good.

---

[22] "Chicagoland", Chicago Tribune, 15th November 2011.

Financial Management

Financial rules are financial rules … at least they are to innocent minds.

In the Muslim World

Muhammad, in the *Constitution of Medina* in 622, imposed a 'head tax' (*jizya*) on Christians, Jews and Zoroastrians in Muslim countries as a fee for protection by the Muslim state.[23] [24]

In theory, later converts to Islam were then freed of the obligation of the tax. However, the tax was so profitable that Caliphs after Muhammad were very reluctant to give up any part of such a lucrative income. So more and more local officials simply 'forgot' to exempt new converts from the tax, which they were encouraged to keep on paying.

Belgium

In 2011, a supplicant discovered that he was entitled to interest on taxes that had been overcharged and which were not recovered for over a year. He was not told of any entitlement, so the interest would simply have been absorbed by the Flemish authorities if he had not taken the initiative and invoiced the state for 5%. In fact he was entitled to 7% of the refunded overcharge.

He eventually got it. Persistence pays.

---

[23] Wikipedia, Jizya, http://en.wikipedia.org/wiki/Jizya

[24] *"The History of the Medieval World,'* Susan Wise Bauer, W.W. Norton, 2010, p. 357.

Not much has changed in 1389 years. In both cases the tax inspectors were civil servants acting under direction from the government. Presumably one of their instructions was to not volunteer legal prerogatives in favor of the applicant.

British Capital Gains Tax

DH relates an example of high handedness exhibited by a minor civil servant operating only according to rule, or at least his interpretation of a rule.

The formula used by the United Kingdom Inland Revenue to value the 'wealth' of a citizen contemplating emigration, so that a Capital Gains Tax Demand (15% of that 'wealth') can be issued before emigration, is (or at least was) as follows.

In this case, there was very little real money involved. However, DH had several patents through which he was willing to allow British manufacturers to improve their processes and lines. He started with an exclusive licensing agreement for use of one of his patents in Scotland.

According to the agreement the Licensee was to pay a yearly royalty of £30,000 per year to DH. That was fair reward for the new efficient cost-saving process that he had invented.

The value of that License Agreement of exclusive rights in Scotland was taken into consideration by the tax official for the computation of Capital Gains Tax. One might think that Capital Gains Tax would be annually payable on £30,000.

However, the tax official argued thus: since Scotland has 10% of the British population, the 'guaranteed minimum' Scottish payment of £30,000 had to be multiplied by 10 to represent income in Britain. Therefore he estimated DH's yearly British royalty income at £300,000, even though there was no exclusive licensing agreement other than in Scotland and no legitimate reason to expect an additional £270,000 a year coming from anywhere.

He then applied a term of ten-years' income from any individual patent agreement so the British patent was estimated to raise a total of £3,000,000 … if it were exclusive to the whole of Britain and if it brought in the same pro-rated income for ten years.

"How many patents have you had been granted?" asked the Tax Official. DH told him thirty-six. The tax official then multiplied £3,000,000 by 36 and declared that, "the value of your British patents is one hundred and eight million pounds." This assumed of course that each patent was worth the same and that rights to each could be sold at all.

He continued, "The Capital Gains Tax on £108,000,000, at 15%, is £16,200,000. If you pay this amount of tax before you emigrate you will be free to return to the UK whenever you wish. No further tax will be due. However, if the tax is not paid, you may leave the country, but, if you ever return, you will immediately be imprisoned for evading tax".

The civil servant charged with helping a citizen had estimated his version of **probable** earnings but he demanded **real** money in tax. There is a difference! Furthermore, the tax official knew full well that DH's annual income would only be £30,000 if payments started.

It is hard not to suspect that this official, with a rule in his holster, was merely being malicious and that it might be an individual case. However, experience shows that this individual cavalier lordship happens time and time again.

On one hand DH, having earned nothing yet from his patents, did not have £16,200,000 to pay anything. On the other, he needed to visit England frequently to visit his retired and ailing father.

So he asked, "Is it only on the basis of the Scottish License Agreement that you demand £16,200,000 from me?" The civil servant said "yes" and he elaborated, "No License Agreement, no Tax Demand". So, DH 'tore up' the License Agreement and then asked him, "How much do I now owe in Capital Gains Tax?" The tax servant replied, "You now owe the British government nothing and are free to emigrate, and return whenever you choose".

At the time that the exclusive license agreement had been signed in Scotland, DH was already negotiating an exclusive license agreement in England with one of the largest Precast Concrete Manufacturers. They, in preparation for the "signing", had already provisionally ordered eight new machines, designed according to the patent specification.

All eight machines would be in use full time according to the License Agreement. Two of these machines in Poole, Dorset; two in Malvern; two in Leicestershire and the other two in the north of England. The machines would be made in Dewsbury, near to Leeds in Yorkshire. Also, DH was negotiating an Exclusive License in Northern Ireland, and, still had Wales to consider.

In total, in retrospect it was estimated that DH's UK annual royalty income might exceed £10,000,000. Then using the official's formula of estimating his worth, it would be £3,600 million (£10,000,000 x 36 x 10) and he might owe 15% of this in tax: £540 million. Quite a thought!

Here the civil servant only complied with rules, perhaps maliciously. Even though he sat back with his eyes on the ceiling as he delivered the Wisdom of Solomon, he was not bright enough to think, nor even was he empowered to think, further than the regulation. He never considered, for example, the loss of the patentable work to Britain.

With a little thought the official could have negotiated an acceptable progressive plan of tax payment depending upon receipts -- since nothing is worth anything if no income is received. Instead, he chose the hard line, the simplest line according to his light, and thereby he lost for Britain, a brilliant brain and the British exclusive rights to a number of new technologies.

DH left Britain and has not been back for 35 years. His royalties simply followed him abroad.

Others who dealt with the tax inspectors were more fortunate.

"When I was a tax partner in a large firm ...... I can think of a number of occasions when I sat with a senior representative of the Her Majesty's Revenue and Customs and done a "deal.""[25]

---

[25] "The Times", Friday 23, 2011 Letters to the Editor, Julian Pilcher, Steventon, Hants, UK

John Graham

Belgian Tax Rules

A slightly different example: through a clerical error of a civil servant, compounded by lack of cooperation between government departments, a car owner was charged 1,108.94 euros too much to get his imported car onto Belgian roads.

Another civil servant at the Ministry of Transport explained that although she knew of the error, he would have to pay the whole amount that he had been invoiced on the books before it could be adjusted. After he paid, she explained that it would then take approximately four months to get a refund. This was in September 2010.

Then, on January 1st 2011, the responsibility was shifted from the Federal Ministry of Transport to the Flanders Regional Ministry who claimed to know nothing of the matter until an Ombudsman was involved. This ignorance was claimed despite registered letters that had been sent and received months before. The refund had, by then, been owed for eight months. The civil servant contacted by the Ombudsman first stated that they had 45 days to consider the issue … they then took 39 days to write to say that they usually attempted to solve financial claims of this sort within six months.

The clock was still ticking in October 2011 while the government earned interest on its overcharge.

Much of this delay could be attributed to inefficiency, but some is due to the civil servant's objection to oversight by an Ombudsman. Certainly, the plaintiff has no rights. If the government servant cannot see the plaintiff, he doesn't exist. He is merely an imposition in the workday. However, an ombudsman looks over one's shoulder.

Belgium has another financial issue in common with several other European states. The country supports so much government that its taxation is very high indeed. A typical professional will hand back 52% of his income in tax. Furthermore, when his wife goes shopping she pays a purchase tax (the BTW or "Belasting over de Toegevoegde Waarde") of 21%. All this taxation is used to fund the government and social services. The interface between those who administer the government taxation and services and the public are civil servants.

The taxation is so high that typically it is avoided whenever possible. People buy consumer goods abroad where the added tax is lower or they employ the black market, especially when labor is bought. In the latter case, if one pays in cash and do not need a receipt, there is no need to pay the 21% BTW. The transaction benefits both the seller and the buyer.

The odd thing about this arrangement is that civil and government servants with the responsibility of administering the BTW taxation are just as likely to use the black market when they are not at the office.

A television repair man offered the 'cash and no receipt' illegal convenience to his customers and often was able to accommodate the police when their television sets went sour. On those occasions he had a different relationship with civil servants than when they operated within business hours. The actual individuals had not changed but their environment had. For one thing, they stood in front of a counter rather than behind it.

Private companies

Another example, United Airlines, as a cost saving measure, employs inexpensive labor in India for their Customer Relations' staff. They 'outsource'. One can tell to whom one is speaking because all the Indian clerks sound like the comedian, Peter Sellers, imitating an Indian.

The person who 'represents' the United Airlines Company on the phone might have little or no understanding of what an U.S. passenger flying through Chicago has had to experience. Instead they deal from a standard set of 'Questions and Answers.' They are very polite and patient. They have to be because they are rarely able to satisfy a complaint.

Indeed, trying to get answers from this outsourced customer-relations group is like dealing with marshmallow. They accept all manner of enquiries but can never provide a definitive answer. At best they advise that you can write to Corporate Customer Relations in Chicago. No, they have no phone number or e-mail address for 'Corporate Customer Relations.'

The experience is worse that dealing with an uncaring and inefficient government servant in a home office.

Which is perhaps why one long-term flier with close to two million miles of flying and seven years in the top echelon of 'Mileage-plus' passengers now makes his bookings with Lufthansa.

Another American example:

Wells Fargo is a well-known U.S. banking institution and they announced proudly in 2008 that they were instituting Internet banking so that money could be transferred and bills paid on line. It sounded good.

However, after dealing *ad nauseum* with 'Banking Advisors' in a Colorado branch it was apparent that they really did not know how money transfer worked on line. Apparently, in their mind it only worked when you came to the branch in person to send money. Their concept of Internet banking didn't extend to it being done from home. Their solution was to promise an investigation and "we'll call you right back." That never happened.

Eventually, it became apparent that all International transfers were done through a branch of the bank on the West Coast and it would only work if you PHONED **within their working hours** and had in your possession three different identity and password numbers. Moreover, these numbers automatically became defunct in three months. A transfer could not be managed from your computer even though you could happily buy goods and pay by credit card instantly in non-banking institutions.

Over the course of six months no money was transferred successfully through the Wells Fargo Bank "modern Internet system" and not one voice representative was the least bit concerned with their failure. The failure, to their mind, was apparently due to something that the customer had not done correctly.

John Graham

Security – managing protection

In the Netherlands

When DH and his wife moved to Putte in the
Netherlands some time ago, the town, of about 4,000
inhabitants, had it's own Police Station and five full
time policemen. The locals felt safe and were pleased
with the service. About ten years ago, as a "cost
saving" measure, the local Police Station was closed
and four of the staff were moved nine kilometers to a
larger town with a population of about 10,000.

That was very inconvenient, and, Putte suffered more
vandalism because the police were remote. For
example, when DH telephoned the police to report
vandalism **in progress** by eight youths at the local
Tennis Club he was 'told' to drive to the police station,
nine kilometers away, to make a report.

Then the police became remoter. When DH telephoned
the police to make an appointment to have his
signature on a legal document witnessed, he was
informed that the police station had been closed and
that he was talking to the police now sixty-kilometers
away in Tilburg.

In Belgium

The same thing happens elsewhere. The police in
Hoogstraten, Belgium, who during the day act merely
as meter maids, go off duty at 5:00 p.m. Then security
for the town, such as it is, is handled from another
station in Turnhout, 20 kilometers away. Thus,
Hoogstraten boasts 14,000 residents and 100,000 in
the surrounding area without a full-time police force.

However, the police, when on duty, have apparently been imbued with a sense of importance. One policeman who was supposed to be on traffic duty at a dangerous junction but who instead cowered on the sidewalk, said, "I'm the boss here. The children listen to me." That is not unusual and it indicates very clearly that your problems are not theirs despite the fact that a policeman is a public servant and is charged with acting on behalf of the public. Instead a sense of 'being in charge' intervenes.

There is one crucial pedestrian crossing that is used several times a day by the children of the Kleine Seminairie on one side of the road. The children, the youngest at two and a half with parents, but ranging all the way up to the teens, on foot and on bikes, come to school at 7:30 a.m., leave at midday and leave again in late afternoon. The street is used by a mass of traffic including an almost continuous convoy of large semis taking a short cut from the Netherlands to central Belgium.

These trucks do not want to stop for a pedestrian crossing, thus parents have organized a protective watch to conduct the children across the road.

… And the police?

While they are willing to "train" the volunteers, they are not willing to take responsibility for the crossing in the midst of traffic. This is even when the traffic is more suited to the throughways than to a town center. Instead, the 'police' would prefer to monitor parking.

Now, a woman was killed crossing for a bus stop and a small girl has been killed at an adjacent crossing. There were no police in attendance.

On another occasion, at another entrance to a school, parking was prohibited for a day for road repairs on a third entrance. It happened to be wet. The school was forced to provide parking direction by teacher volunteers while the police sat watching, dry inside a police van.

The Hoogstraten police are the epitome of local government servants who have lost the respect of the community they are supposed to serve. I suspect they are not very different from other local police in Belgium.

However, the problem is larger than these ineffectual public servants.

Speaking of national safety issues, in the battle for regional power, as a Government is being formed for Belgium after two years of being without one, regional politicians have raised all manner of specious issues and have no concern over harming the security of the population.

The bones of contention this time include the regionalization of the Highway Code, the Fire Service and the Civil Defence Corps. This is despite the well-documented evidence that splitting responsibilities for these functions between different areas of the country is a danger to the public. They would then be forced to use the dominant language of their region. The only real issue here is how much power the French and Flemish negotiators can say they walked away with. They are public servants but both groups are at fault. It would be interesting to know how they justify squabbling between each other in the role of acting for the public.

In the United States

A driver received a fine for speeding in the mail. It was based on a radar reading.

The driver was sure that he had not exceeded a speed limit since he was traveling a very short distance (less than a mile) and carrying a very valuable and fragile cargo – the family's Christmas wine and liqueur supply.

He elected to go to court and he took the aggressive line. Before the date he requested both the radar device instruction manual and the training log for the police officer involved.

On the court date, before the appearance in court he had the opportunity to meet with the officer's superior. In questioning he found that the officer had never received training in the use of the radar equipment but had been provided with the manual, which was, it was claimed, very simple. The captain was clearly a bit concerned that the lack of training would be revealed.

In court the driver had the opportunity to question the officer. Under questioning, the officer did not know the humidity on the day in question. Nor did he know that humidity, according to the manual, affected the accuracy of the radar readings. Nor, he admitted, had he ever received training in the use of the Japanese equipment.

The speeding summons was summarily dismissed.

You **can** question the decision of the civil servant, in this case, the police officer, involved.

Back in Belgium

However, that might not work.

A registered complaint regarding how a police officer failed to effectively control a traffic junction and how his response to being questioned had been unacceptable from a public servant ("F*ck off" was all he could manage) was answered by a department telephone call. While the captain was conciliatory and admitted a problem nothing was put on paper. The captain said that police officer was due to be interviewed following the complaint.

However, nothing happened so a second registered letter was sent. This again received a telephone call. Again an interview of the offending officer was promised.

Again nothing happened. It would have taken the use of legal counsel to get satisfaction so the third registered letter noted that the matter had been dropped but the file including transcripts of phone conversations remained open for any further problem with this particular police officer.

He has not been seen in town since. It might be a coincidence but it is hoped that he received at least an earful.

Times past and times abroad

No nation can claim that its government servants are different from another's either now or in past times. Moreover there is always the issue of what to do about one's grievances inside and outside of the civil service.

In Ancient China

A young man, Huang Chao, known for his intelligence and his literary abilities since childhood, took a civil service examination in 874 and failed.[26]   He was furious. He was convinced that the examination was simply a tool of exclusion especially since there had been prior complaints.

He turned outlaw and south of the Yellow River he began to sell salt illegally, thus breaking a government monopoly. He was joined my other malcontents who became a Robin Hood band. As troops were sent against him, his army grew to half a million and eventually the Emperor fled leaving Huang Chao in control of the capital city of Chang'an. He declared himself king of a new dynasty in 880 and wasn't defeated for another four years.

This is perhaps one of the earliest examples of an embryo supplicant objecting to the regulations. There are very few modern examples of opposition to the government civil service except during the French Revolution in 1789 and in bankrupt Greece in 2011 when civil service jobs were at stake.

---

[26] "The History of the Medieval World," Susan Wise Bauer, W.W. Norton, New York, 2010, p. 415-416

Nevertheless, even civil servants can rebel against government policy. From the outside it is more difficult.

Pre-Nazi Germany

So here he was, at the headquarters of the Health Insurance Fund.[27] It was one those extraordinarily impressive head office buildings with a porter, a giant entrance hall and artistically designed counters.

So along came the little man, Pinneberg. He entered the huge, resplendent, luminous building, wanting his hundred marks, or maybe as much as a hundred and twenty. He had no idea how much might be left over after the hospital charges had been deducted. He stood in the mammoth hall, as small and shabby a figure as you could wish for. The building seemed to say, 'Pinneberg, my dear man! Are a hundred marks really so important to you? We deal in millions here, and your hundred marks are of no importance to us whatever. They have no role in our scheme of things. That's to say, they do have a role, but let's not talk about that at the moment. True this building was erected from the contributions of people just as small as you, but we'd rather you didn't think too much about that. We use your contributions exactly as we are permitted to do by law.'

It was something of a comfort to Pinneberg to see employees like himself siting behind the counter: they could be his colleagues. Otherwise he would have

---

[27] "Little man, what now?" Hans Falada, translated by Susan Bennett, Melville House Classics, 2009, first published by Rowohlt, Berlin, 1932. Pp. 230-231.

been quite overpowered by all this noble wood and stone.

Pinneberg looked keenly around. Over there was the right counter: with the initial P. A young man was sitting there, thankfully not behind bars, just on the other side of the counter.

"Pinneberg." Said Pinneberg. "Johannes. Membership number: 606867. My wife has had a baby, and I've come about the Confinement and Nursing Mothers' ...".

The young man was busy with a card index. He didn't have time to look up. But he stretched out a hand and said, "Membership card."

"Here," said Pinneberg. "I wrote to you ...'.

"Birth certificate." Said the young man, stretching his hand out again.

Pinneberg said mildly: "Excuse me, I wrote to you. I sent you the forms I got from the hospital."

The young man looked up. He looked at Pinneberg: "So what d'you want then?"

"I want to know whether it has been dealt with. Whether the money has been sent. I need it."

"So do we all."

Pinneberg asked, even more mildly: "Has the money been sent to me?"

"I don't know." Said the young man. "If you applied by post it will be dealt with by post."

"Could you perhaps find out whether it has been dealt with?"

"Everything's dealt with promptly here."

"But it ought to have come yesterday."

"Why yesterday? How do you know?"

"I worked it out. If it's been dealt with promptly.'

"You worked it out! How could you know the way things are handled here? There are various sections."

"If it's been dealt with promptly..."

"Everything's dealt with promptly here, you can be sure of that."

Pinneberg said gently but firmly: "So please could you find out whether it has been dealt with or not?"

The young man looked at Pinneberg. Pinneberg looked at the young man. Both of them were smartly dressed. Pinneberg was obliged to look respectable in his job. Both of them had washed and shaved, both had clean nails and both of them were white-collar workers.

But they were enemies, deadly enemies, because one of them was sitting behind a counter and the other was standing in front. The one wanted what he considered to be his rights; the other regarded it as an imposition.

"Lot of fuss about nothing," grumbled the young man. But as Pinneberg continued to fix him with his eye he got up and disappeared into the background. There was a door there, and the young man went in. Pinneberg watched him go. On the door was a sign, and Pinneberg's eyes were not good enough to be able *to read the writing on it for certain, but the longer he looked, the more convinced he was that it said, "Toilets."*

Pinneberg was enraged. A yard away sat another young man, under the letter 'O'. Pinneberg would have liked to ask him about the toilets, but it would have been no use. O would be just the same as P. They were on one side of the counter: he was on the other.

After a fairly long time, actually a very long time, the young man reappeared through the same door, which Pinneberg was fairly certain had 'Toilets' written on it.

Pinneberg looked eagerly at him, but the young man did not look back. He sat down, picked up Pinneberg's membership card, laid it on the counter and said, "Dealt with."

"The money's been sent? Yesterday or today?"

"I told you. It's been dealt with by post."

"When, please?"

"Yesterday."

Pinneberg looked at the young man again. It was very fishy; that had definitely been the 'Toilets.' "If I don't find the money at home, ..." he threatened.

But the young man had finished with him. He was speaking to his opposite number, the man at 'O,' about 'funny people'.

The time: 1930-31, in Berlin during the German period of horrendous inflation before the Nazis came to power, when everyone was desperately poor. Pinneberg knew that a hundred marks was almost three months rent or a pram for his new son.

Nothing has changed in 80 years in across the world: young men still sit behind counters thinking that the supplicant before them is an imposition on their time. The only change today is that young women have generally replaced the young men.

That wasn't the end of this story of course in 1930, for, just as in a similar case in the U.S. in 1995, requirements followed requirements: proof that Pinneberg and his wife had been insured for the previous two years, proof of their own ages and marriage, official town-hall proof confirming the birth of their child rather than confirmation from the hospital, proof of their own health and the length of the mother's pregnancy, proof of employment and so on and on. Each requirement met the job description of yet another disinterested civil servant who had the responsibility of filing that particular piece of information. No one had any interest in the couple's dire need of the money that they were owed.

Hans Fallada's tale is fiction but its circumstances occur every day the world over. Don't you recognize it?

Poland 1979

Another example comes from Poland in 1979.

A visitor arriving in Warsaw from Moscow by Aeroflot wanted simply to stay overnight before catching an American plane to the United States. He knew that he could obtain a short-term visa at immigration offices in the airport.

It was possible, but it sure wasn't quick. It took several hours for a single clerk to process a single application. Most of the time seemed to be taken by the clerk sitting silently at a desk on one side of a barrier, while I, the applicant, sat silently on the other side. There was no one else around, no other applicants and no other clerks. My passport and the application lay in front of him on the desk. After a suitable time, while he fiddled with other papers, he signed the application, stamped it and the passport several times with different stamps, and then called me over to hand it back. After that I was free to get currency changed, and then to start the search for a cab to the city and a hotel for the night. [28]

It turned out that I should have been more patient and asked for more pieces of paper to be duly signed and stamped by all concerned, perhaps at another airport office.

The visit over-night was a success. I sampled 24 hours of Warsaw life; slept, ran, ate, walked through the old town and along the river, and shopped. In due course I returned to the airport for my next flights to Hamburg and to the U.S.

All was well until I came to the Polish Customs. The customs lady was obviously an accomplished weight lifter -- in the heavyweight class -- certainly not a person upon whom you would practice Polish jokes. She was happily mishandling people's baggage on a long steel counter leading to the security gate for the flights. Each passenger would laboriously lift his or

---

[28] *"Snapshots of the Mind"*, John Graham, Publish America, 2005, pp. 25 et seq.

her case onto the counter and the customs lady would flip it over with one hand while she glared at its owner. Passengers were, without exception, meek before her.

I was meek too.

I offered my cases: my soft-sided running bag and my camera case. She ignored them and said something guttural and unintelligible. It couldn't have been in my phrase book. I looked politely quizzical. More guttural sounds and this time something, which ended in "paper". I had to remain quizzical -- "currency paper" -- and I remembered the system in the Soviet Union.

There everything valuable had to be declared on entry and then checked with receipts on exit. This female Goliath was asking for that currency form -- something I had not obtained on entry 24 hours earlier. I tried to explain, realizing that the affair of getting a temporary visa had forced me to enter the country separated from the normal passengers and somehow this vital form had not been completed.

I didn't have it. I said so. She said that I had to have it. She also said, "Without paper you can not leave," this time in English as clear as a bell, and she swept me aside, away from her counter. I was apparently dispatched as being unqualified to leave Poland, and that was that. She had no suggestions. It looked as though I might be in trouble.

I stood my ground in front of her with fast disappearing courage.

"It is not my fault."

"Without paper you can not leave."

She turned to the next passenger and started checking luggage again. However, my bags were in the way and she tried to push them off the counter towards me. I pushed them back. She pushed them away. I pushed them back. I wasn't as strong, but I was persistent. There was a low gentle mumbling from the passengers behind me who realized that they might miss their flights if this crazy American, who didn't know enough to have the right papers, wasn't cleared quickly.

As my robust customs lady and I traded pushes with my luggage, the mumbling got louder and more distinct. It could have been as much against me, as for me, but it did the trick. My heavyweight opponent realized that I could be more trouble than I was worth. I threatened to extend her workday. She threw her hefty arms to the sky -- glared at me -- and, impatiently, waved me on. If I had been standing where her arm swept forward I would have been hefted right past the next security check. I was on my way again.

But I could have still been there!

United States 1996

1. *"Welcome to the United States of America. We hope that you enjoy your visit. Here's your passport. Just walk to your right for customs. Have a good day."*

2. *"Why are you coming to the U.S.? What do you think you are going to get here?" and flinging them on the floor, "Take your papers."*

3. *"Welcome back home."*

Greetings from the same types of immigration officers at the incoming airport: the three different approaches were results of the status of the incoming passenger and unthinking government clerks.

In the first case, the passenger was a visitor. In the second, she had applied for permanent resident status for entry and, therefore, had an I-94 form, and in the third case she was either a qualified permanent alien or a citizen. At the time when you do not need a hassle with any US authority, when you have 'probationary' status, immigration officers are typically disrespectful and like to exercise their power. They know that you have none.

That is not only true in this case but regularly. Worse greetings were given to a newcomer who obviously did not know the finer details of entry into the U.S. such as "standing behind the yellow line until called for." I have heard a female immigration clerk snarl, "Get back behind the yellow line. Can't you read?"

Immigration officials typically know their power and they like to use it.

On another occasion, a woman passenger, after a nine-hour trans-Atlantic flight and being unfamiliar with regulations, completed an I-94 incoming form mistakenly giving her U.S. address in place of her parents' European one.[29] She was quickly shunted to a holding room, thus ensuring that she and her husband would miss the connecting domestic flight. There,

---

[29] You cannot use your U.S. address until you have alien residency status even though you are entitled to live in the U.S. while you wait and, indeed, may have no other address.

other immigration officials refused to listen to her and simply told her to wait in line ... while they chatted.

Fortunately, her husband had both U.S. and British citizenship. Being a Brit he harbored no illusions about minions, whatever badge they wore. He demanded to see their superior.

Their response, "We don't have a superior," drew the husband's snort of laughter, and a very firm request that they find one immediately since they were mere clerks and they had better do it NOW.

"He's somewhere out on the immigration floor."

The husband stormed out, accosted the first immigration officer and demanded to see his superior. The superior was there in seconds, heard the complaint and walked back with the husband into the holding room. The wife was released immediately with apologies ... in time for the flight connection.

The original immigration officer and the two in the holding room were countermanded, but it took status and demonstrative anger to do it. That should not be needed.

Canadian Experiences

A much earlier example involved a demure old lady in her late seventies visiting the U.S.A. from Britain. She was on a day trip with her son to Niagara Falls in Canada. She presented her passport to the Canadian immigration officer in Buffalo and he asked her were she had come from. She proudly replied, "America." It was her first visit.

In response, he snarled, "We are 'America' too." Then he proceeded to give the poor old lady a lecture on the use of the word 'America' to represent a continent rather than a country and that the U.S.A. was not 'America.' He threw her passport back at her.

That encounter with the first Canadian she had met on her visit to the country spoiled her day and left her with a nasty taste in her mouth about the courtesy of Canadians.

An unthinking jingoistic individual should not serve as an immigration officer.

On another Canadian occasion, a person attending a scientific meeting on Long Island had been given half a bottle of local wine as a gift. On his return to Ottawa through Toronto, he was summarily told by customs that he hadn't stayed out of the country long enough to bring in half a bottle of wine without duty. The duty would be a percentage of its cost.

"It was free. I have no idea of its value."

"You must estimate it – it has some value."

He said, "OK, I don't want it. You can drink it."

"No, no! We can't accept it."

His response totally embarrassed the customs officers (there were two) and they tried to force him to keep the wine and pay the duty at some presumed cost. The response that he would willingly pour it out into a garbage can and carry the empty bottle was also more than they could accept. Finally, he left it on the ground and went through customs without it.

It was an example of two Canadian customs officers (civil servants) who could only operate to rule. They didn't even consider the stupidity of a rule, which demanded a percentage of the cost of a free half-bottle of wine because the owner had only stayed outside the country for a day.

The custom's officers of any reasonable country would have waved the article through. Instead, these civil servants labeled their country as the home of fools.

Utter Pradesh, India

A snake charmer in India released 40 poisonous snakes, including a number of cobras, onto the floor of a Government Land Registry Office to protest the delay of a new land permit.[30]

Hakkul also accused bureaucrats in the northern Indian state of Uttar Pradesh of demanding bribes for his land application:

"I am a conservationist and have been seeking the government's help. Having waited patiently for so long, I had no option but to leave all my snakes in this office," Hakkul said he received promise of a land permit two years ago so that he would have a place for his snakes to live.

The government says it has continued to delay Hakkul's request because snake charmers are illegal.

"He had applied for a plot of land to keep his snakes," Subhash Mani Tripathi, the head of land-revenue administration. "But there is no provision for such a business. Instead of seeking a written reply, which we

---

[30] Yahoo News from the U.K. Guardian, Telegraph and AFP, December 5, 2011

would have issued, Hakkul created panic by letting loose a bunch of snakes all over the office."

He certainly got those civil servants' interest and attention.

Mandating what is good for you

Politicians often take it upon themselves to administer society for 'your' betterment without a clear mandate to do so. Their civil servants in turn believe their jobs are a form of religion and that serving the public is merely a matter of ensuring the public does what it is told, not what it wants. Civil service in this way is turned upon its head. It becomes a disservice.

Green Laws

Green laws are a fine example of irrational behaviour by extreme government servants.

The U.S. Environmental Protection Agency (EPA) regulates according to the lowest level of any pollutant that it can measure rather than down to a level that has been shown to be harmful. Thus, recently the agency proposed tightening up its anti-smog laws, which included a curtailment of any measureable ozone. It acted out of a supposed care of the environment and a supposed connection between ozone levels and global warming, even though the latter has been disproved.

As required by law the agency conducted a value study and came to the conclusion that the new regulations would cost $90 billion per year -- to be borne by business. In return they expected to recoup $100 billion a year 'in benefits' by the year 2020. The costs are known, the benefits are 'expected' apparently from lengthening the lives of asthmatics. The facts are that the benefits were entirely specious. However, the sum was not meant to balance: the costs are borne by business and ultimately the consumer while the benefits are paid into government.

In this case President Obama wisely quashed the proposed regulation in September 2011. Of course that incurred huge criticism by the agency civil servants, by green lobbyists and by those who would have gained from the enforcement.

Other EPA regulations have not had the benefit of considered opinion and action.

Radiation Protection

The U.S. Nuclear Regulatory Commission has the same philosophy: regulate to the smallest amount measurable. However, they also violate known science.

There is good evidence to show that low levels of radiation are beneficial to the human body[31] while high levels are harmful, much as one aspirin will cure your headache while a hundred taken together will kill you. Yet the Commission continues to regulate to the lowest possible measurement, saying, 'any radiation is harmful.'

This incurs huge costs and harm to those who might benefit from low doses. It also has created a Commission of the U.S. government filled with government servants who believe they are forcing

---

[31] **Effects of Low Doses of Radiation:**
D Boreham, McMaster University, Canada, A Brooks, Washington State University Tri-Cities, USA, D J Higson, Australian Nuclear Association, Australia, Y-C Luan, Nuclear Biological and Chemical Protection Society, Taiwan, R E Mitchel, Atomic Energy of Canada Ltd, Canada, J. Strzelczyk, University of Colorado at Denver, Radiology, USA, and P Sykes, Flinders University and Medical Centre, Australia, Joint statement at the 15th Pacific Basin Nuclear Conference, Sydney, Australia, October 2006.

good on the U.S. population, while in reality they do the reverse.

One of the worst ideas is to regulate radon in your basement. The levels reached are actually beneficial so that you could no better than sleep there. However the scares issued by the Commission, which has no mandate to regulate your home, are so persuasive that it affects the sale of houses.[32] It is quite common that the seller be asked to pay for a basement radon pump and of course manufacturers of radon pumps are delighted to add to the misinformation. They distribute leaflets to show how harmful radon is.

Unfortunately, health physicists, as servants of the government, swear by their philosophy that no level of radiation is safe. Of course if this were not their assertion they would most probably be out of a job.

Transportation Safety

Those of us who travel internationally have been provided with mandatory 'protection' against terrorist activities on planes.

The first use of baggage checking occurred after a number of planes were hi-jacked and diverted, then the 'protection' provided in the United States went into paranoid overdrive following the September 9th 2001 destruction of the New York Trade Towers, the attack on the Pentagon and a diverted attack on another

---

[32] My response in two house sales is to say "No" to any radon remediation and to provide a wealth of learned information showing that a little radon is beneficial. The issue then has gone away, perhaps because of my credentials as a former President of the American Nuclear Society.

John Graham

Washington target. None of the 19 attackers were detected as they boarded four planes with weapons even though the regulations were already in force.

Unfortunately, neither has a terrorist been detected since, even though the methods of 'protection' have got steadily more intrusive over the years. Each time an undetected incident occurs new regulations are imposed. The agencies involved are very adept at closing stable doors. Checking shoes is one of these stable doors.

Baggage is X-rayed and a number of articles are forbidden in carry-on items for the flight. Passengers, even children, are submitted to questioning and searching, shoes and belts are removed and full body X-rays are used randomly as well as in the event of any doubt. Full-body frisking, including the thrusting of a hand inside one's trousers and then down one's belly and up into one's groin, is the latest of the intrusive methods of 'protecting' the passenger. The agency calls this violation a 'pat-down' procedure but to many of the employees it's a 'feel-up' procedure. It goes along with their laughter at full-body images from the electronic scanners.

When this inspection was first established a host of individuals were hired, mostly from the ranks of the unemployed. It showed. They were the least employable of people and, naturally, not the brightest. However, typically, the government employee has been told that he or she is the savior of national security. You, as an airline user, have no rights and the slightest objection could quickly lose you your plane and worse. The police stand adjacent to the inspection sites at all times, ready to arrest. It is reminiscent of 14th Century policing and summary incarceration.[33]

The relationship between the passenger and the authoritarian inspector got so bad that the agency … in the United States it is the Transport Security Administration (TSA) … made an effort to improve the civility of their employees. They had training. Posters were erected stating that inspectors would be civil and do everything they could to protect the privacy of the passenger. That was a total failure as the inspectors retained the idea that they were little 'gods.' When they have fingered you, their final words are often an insulting, "Have a good day."

You can of course complain through the TSA e-mail address. Here is the reply:

"Transportation Security Administration's Office of Civil Rights and Liberties. In the event that you have reached our office in error, and have a claim or general question, we are automatically forwarding your concern to the TSA Contact Center for appropriate handling."

"However, if you believe that you have been discriminated against by a Transportation Security Officer (TSO) at an airport checkpoint, please respond directly to this email message."

"Please provide us with the following additional information: (1) date and approximate time of the incident, (2) location of the incident, (3) name of the air carrier, (4) the badge number(s), name(s), or

---

[33] Ian Mortimer, "The Time Traveler's Guide to Medieval England," Simon and Schuster, New York, 2010, Chapter 10

description(s) of the TSO(s) involved, and (5) a statement (200 words or less) describing what occurred, the basis of discrimination, and why you believed this constituted discriminatory treatment. This additional information will assist us in our review of your concern. Thank you for bringing this matter to our attention."

The enquiry that TSA was sent concerned their Codes of Conduct for their employees, so this response was largely irrelevant. If the enquiry e-mail was forwarded it clearly reached a black hole. There has been no response.

The following TSA experience is not untypical in showing the mentality of these inspectors who are civil servants.

A young woman with 18-month-old twin daughters was traveling from Denver to Brussels. It is a very long flight with a connection through Washington, DC, so she had taken the precaution of bringing a sealed container of fresh milk for each girl, since this is not available on planes. To satisfy the TSA inspectors she also had a signed recommendation from the girls' physician for the milk. Prescribed food had been allowed in the past.

This time it wasn't. The inspector surveying the mother and her babies in a stroller demanded that the bottles were opened and the milk tasted by the mother. She naturally refused. There was only just enough milk for the toddlers on the 12-hour journey.

A supervisor was called and her decision was that either the mother was to open the containers and drink the milk or the mother would be subject to a full body search.

Supposedly, the inspection was to detect fluids that could be used as explosives. It's worth noting that a full body search was not an alternative method of testing the milk … it was merely a personal threat.

Yet, both the inspector and her supervisor said they were protecting the public and that the mother should be pleased that they did their job well.

Lest you think this is exaggeration, here's another example from late 2011.

A business consultant, Lori Dorn, was heading from New York to San Francisco. She reported afterwards that the pat down at John F. Kennedy International Airport added, "insult to injury and caused me a great deal of humiliation."

Dorn was passing through TSA 'security' when a full-body scanner detected her breast prostheses. Dorn said she explained to the agent that she had recently undergone bilateral mastectomy and had tissue expanders implanted for future breast reconstruction.

Dorn asked the agent if she could retrieve a medical card from her pocket, which described the expanders and included contact information for her doctor. But the agent called over a supervisor who denied the request, and said the breast exam had to take place. "I had no choice but to allow an agent to touch my breasts in front of other passengers," Dorn said.

Dorn later received an apology from a JFK official "who agreed that proper policy wasn't followed."

The TSA said later that it regretted the incident.

"We do our best to treat passengers with the dignity and respect they deserve, but in Lori Dorn's case, it looks like we missed our mark," it said.[34]

They miss their mark every day.

One more example in which the TSA employee and her supervisor showed coordinated ignorance.

"It's not unusual for 17-year-old to find themselves in hot water with the fashion police. But on a flight from Virginia to Florida, Vanessa Gibbs found herself detained by the Transportation Security Administration (TSA) over the appearance of her purse."

"And just to be clear, it wasn't the content inside the purse that the TSA objected to. No, agency officials took exception with the design of a gun on Gibbs' handbag."

"'It's my style, it's camouflage, it has an old western gun on it,' Gibbs told News4Jax.com. Gibbs didn't run into any trouble while traveling north from Jacksonville International Airport. But on her way back home, TSA officials at Norfolk International Airport pulled her aside."

""The inspector said, 'This is a federal offense because it's in the shape of a gun,'" Gibbs said. "I'm like, 'But it's a design on a purse. How is it a federal offense?'""

---

[34] "Breast cancer survivor decries pat-down at JFK", Associated Press, 4th October 2011

"After TSA agents figured out the gun was a fake, Gibbs said, they told her to check the bag or turn it over. By the time security wrapped up the inspection, the pregnant teen missed her flight, and Southwest Airlines sent her to Orlando instead. The changed itinerary created no small amount of anxiety for Gibbs' mother, who was already waiting for her to arrive at the Jacksonville airport.""

""Oh, it's terrifying. I was so upset," said Tami Gibbs, the teen's mom. "I was on the phone all the way to Orlando trying to figure out what was going on with her. It was terrifying.""

"Less terrifying is the actual design on the purse, which is only a few inches in size and hollow. "I carried this from Jacksonville to Norfolk, and I've carried it from Norfolk to Jacksonville," Vanessa said. "Never once has anyone said anything about it until now.""

"Nonetheless, the TSA says the design could be considered a "replica weapon," something that the agency has banned since 2002. Just imagine what would have happened if Gibbs had also been wearing stiletto heels."[35]

Unfortunately, the TSA has NEVER ever once prevented a viable threat to a plane. Events they try to prevent have already happened before the stable door is closed. They have made passengers discard all manner of minor penknives and nail files, cosmetics and drinking water. They have subjected passengers to demeaning personal inspections, roughed up personal luggage and in many instances stolen personal property. They do this day in and day out while sanctimoniously claiming their role as savior of transportation. They are apparently civil servants with a mission to serve the public.

But they consider themselves servants to no one. Thus, an entire book could be filled with examples of unthinking Transportation Security Administration federal employees who deal with the public every day. They are generally callous and act as though they are little gods backed by an equally unthinking supervisor and by 'regulations'. The examples of poor public service behaviour are simply too numerous to spend a lot of text on them.

Another case concerns the Federal Drug Administration (FDA) in the United States. They have issued a draft ruling for dietary supplements saying that all new or changed supplements since 1994 must undergo testing before they can be sold.[36]

---

[35] Jacksonville 4 News, December 3, 2011

[36] "Guidance for Industry: Dietary Supplements: New Dietary Ingredient Notifications and Related Issues,"

The regulatory issue is nominally safety although only a single death has occurred in the past 17 years. Since the cost of testing new ingredients to statistical certainty is so high, time-consuming and cumbersome the manufacturers immediately protested. It could put some smaller firms out of business.

In this case there are two issues. Why have some firms been selling products that have apparently not been tested quite safely, and why should supplements be regulated anyway?

It's another case of a regulatory agency mandating what is good for you but in this case the public is almost not involved since the industry will have to pay for the cost of testing. It only hurts the public if their particular brand of snake oil becomes unavailable.

One is allowed to make a comment through a phone number or through the Internet. In the latter case one can also get a copy of the proposed regulation, an 86-page document with so much government language and so many inter-relations that it would be impossible for a member of the public to read.

This is the FDA's idea of communication.

In reality, the FDA would prefer no input from the public so although the links are apparently there, no individual communicator is behind any of them.

One can argue with the regulation in detail or in totality. Then the real issue is whether there should be any regulation at all of what an individual chooses to

---

http://www.fda.gov/food/guidancecomplianceregulatoryinformatio n/guidancedocuments/dietarysupplements/ucm257563.htm

eat. In any case a member of the public is not involved because the FDA doesn't want them involved.

The latest FDA crusade is against something new – electronic cigarettes, which they manage to connect to 'death'[37] in the following "

*"e-Cigarettes **may** contain ingredients that are known to be toxic to humans, and **may** contain other ingredients that **may** not be safe. Additionally, these products **may** be attractive to young people and **may** lead kids to try other tobacco products, including conventional cigarettes, which are known to cause disease and **lead to** premature **death**."*

"May – may – may – may – may – lead to -- DEATH."

This is typical logic of a regulator. Furthermore, a regulator judges everything as guilty until proved innocent:

"Those calling for tight regulations on e-cigarettes claim that these devices should be deemed illegal until the proper research trials have been conducted to prove that they're safe."

One might ask whether those in regulation should be judged unemployable until proper research trials have been conducted to prove that they are rational.

Civil servants at the FDA are provided with information such as that in italics above to provide to

---

[37] Electronic Cigarettes,
http://www.fda.gov/NewsEvents/PublicHealthFocus/ucm172906.htm

any enquirer. That is the extent of their knowledge so, in reality, it is no use asking.

The dangers

Responsiveness

We regularly endure immense inefficiency from civil servants, even out of sight in handling our business, which we would not tolerate from any one else. This inefficiency could become the norm of business behavior and we are not encouraged to be any more responsive in our own dealings.

As an example: the U.S. Internal Revenue Service (IRS) is a feared organization even if one has done nothing wrong. Remember that the Chicago mafia Don Al 'Scarface' Capone was not convicted of the murders that he had committed or of his racketeering but merely of the tax he didn't pay on the illegal money that he collected. In 1932 he was sentenced to eleven years but was released after eight with his mind gone. He died of syphilis in 1947.[38]

Thus, when an IRS letter arrives and requires that you respond in x days, one makes every effort to do so even though the clerk has used up half the allowable time by sending the letter initially to an address he or she should have known was outdated.

Recently there was another such case. In April 2011 the IRS wanted to know something about the use of a company car in 2008. Identical questions had been posed following both the 2004 return and the 2007 return with no change in the tax positioning in either case. Now the IRS was back asking the same questions

---

[38] Federal Bureau of Investigation, Famous Cases and Criminals, <http://www.fbi.gov/about-us/history/famous-cases/al-capone>

in 2011 about the 2008 return. Of course, the enquiry was sent to the wrong address so there were just a few days left in which to respond.

They were first told of the mistake in address they had made and what the correct address was and how it would change again on May 1st. They were provided with the information that they had requested and it was pointed out that asking the same questions year after year amounted to harassment. It was suggested that it would be preferable that they settled the issue at their regional office (in Ogden, Utah) rather than force the taxpayer to go over their heads to Washington, DC. That was on April 18th.

Two months later on June 24th and 27th, the IRS sent three letters dated May 9th all to wrong addresses although two of them got the country correct. Two of the letters were identical and explained that they would be responding within 30 days or they would provide a new date for a response. The third letter sent to the wrong country said that they would respond in 45 days.

In late August, a final letter said, "We are pleased to tell you we did not make any changes to the tax reported on your return."

This self same thing had happened in 2009 for the 2007 tax return when delays were announced for three successive 45-day periods. The result was a final letter saying that the matter had been dropped and no changes were made in the tax return. In that case, the IRS was playing for a high stake. If they had been correct I would have been liable to pay an extra $385, far less than it cost the IRS to go through the exercise of collection.

The result of this lack of efficiency is at first regretful laughter ... but we pay these idiots to be 'employed' and to commit the same foolishness, apparently year after year.

This example is from the United States, but the same thing happens elsewhere.

In Belgium, a complaint sent by registered letter, that no one at the Ministry of Finance had responded to valid enquiries, finally got two replies but only when an Ombudsman was involved. One said that they would respond in 45 days and the other from the Ombudsman said that he couldn't even ask questions for 45 days. Moreover, the Ministry defined when the 45 days started ... a month or more after they had received the enquiry.

The parallel delay of 45 days in Europe and in the U.S. seems to show that civil servants talk to each other far more efficiently than they respond to the people they are supposed to serve.

On the other hand, civil servants often respond quickly if they are threatened with the revelation of their personal behaviour. In one case, a civil servant who ignored a request for information since it was not in direct line of her responsibility, immediately responded when she received a communication copied to the Financial Ombudsman and required that the information be supplied within three days 'as per procedure.' You can use 'procedures' in your defence.

The Nez Perce

The Nez Perce Indian tribe of Idaho is an 'Agreement Tribe' because the U.S. Government appropriated their tribal lands at the start of World War II to site a nuclear plant. Hanford, in Washington State went on to manufacture the raw material, which was later separated in Tennessee and made into charges in Colorado before being assembled into nuclear bombs in New Mexico. After the war a massive clean up effort was launched at all these sites and for that at Hanford several Indian tribes had oversight responsibilities, which allowed them to see significant documents relating to the clean up of their lands. The U.S. Government had the responsibility of communicating with the Indian Tribes.[39]

They did so almost maliciously, judging the Nez Perce to be no more than anti-nuclear activists. Instead of sending significant documents and explaining why they were significant, the Government sent **everything** … every piece of paper generated by every committee and project on the site.

The Nez Perce could not complain at not being given information. It came in a flood. It was so voluminous that all they could do was to store it. When this author

---

[39] **The Hanford Tribes**

The Confederated Tribes of the Umatilla Indian Reservation, the **Nez Perce Tribe** and Yakama Nation are important stakeholders with Treaty rights and interests at the Hanford Site. The Department of Energy's environmental cleanup activities have the potential to impact natural and cultural resources and to interfere with American Indian religious practices. Through cooperative agreements, tribal staff and consultants of the tribes are engaged on a daily basis with the government and its contractors. The principle activities by tribes include **reviewing and commenting on plans and documents,** participating in meetings at the request of the government, monitoring cultural resource sites, participating in site surveys, and identifying issues that will require additional consultation with elected officials on a government-to-government level.

http://www.em.doe.gov/tribalpages/initiatives.aspx#siteprogs1

came, as a consultant, to assist in making sense of the paperwork, they literally had a barn full and they had 'lost' the key. They were forced to simply attend meetings and to agree with what was being done.

Department of Energy civil servants always pointed to the fact that they were extremely 'open' and kept nothing from the Indians.

This manner of handling the public reminds one of the child who asks his very busy mother a question only to be told, "Go and ask your Father."

He responds, "No, he always tells me more than I want to know."

United States Government

The U.S. Government is equally guilty today. An Internet site provides access to all those documents, which can currently be reviewed, commented upon and referred to. At the time of writing half a million documents are available to the discriminating reader if he or she is willing to delve into government legalese.[40]

The provision of such an enormous quantity of information can hardly be said to be communication.

However, our usual problem with civil servants is 'less' not 'more.' We can either be ignored, or bucked to another telephone or another office, or sent back to square one for not having the correct forms.

I shudder at the thought because this week includes a visit to a U.S. Embassy to renew the passports for

---

[40] Regulations.gov -- <http://www.regulations.gov/#!home>

four-year-old twins. The requirements include, in addition to applications and fees, photographs to rigid requirements, existing passports, birth certificates, and local residency proofs, father and mother's passports, marriage certificate as well as photo copies of everything and cover forms. In addition everyone has to appear in person with appointments only 15 minutes apart. Since everyone has dual citizenships and the girls are too young to sign anything, the day could be fun. I wouldn't be surprised if the interview also included pat downs.

On the day, a frisking was needed and personal property was removed before access was granted to a clerk who took documents and payment. The final civil servant was genial and quick. Perhaps our preparation helped.

However, preparation didn't help another applicant. He had arrived for pre-arranged interview for a job at the embassy. He was simply turned away. He was given no access to any more knowledgeable person or to the person he had come to see. The clerk simply turned him away, advising him that he had to acquire Belgian papers to do business in Belgium. There was no appeal to her decision other than that he should write a letter.

Learning bad habits

There is another very probable and much more worrisome danger in dealing with civil servants.

While we are irritated, annoyed, and put to extra effort following our encounters with rude and unresponsive public servants, since there are so many of them and contacts are so frequent, this sort of behaviour could become a public norm. Do we behave in the same manner to those who contact us on any matter?

It is easy to brush off enquiries since it requires less effort than considering a proper response. Looking back I can see how easy it is and to realize that we had been guilty ourselves on occasion even with our own children.

Adoption

What follows is a personal story. In it the individuals meet public servants on all kinds, both those working for small companies, those working for institutions and those working for governments of different types and nationalities. The motives of these public servants differ, as do their approaches and responses to the individuals in the story.

The reader will be able to see those who care for the process and those who care for themselves and those who care for regulations. They are all here

Adoption is a complex process involving all manner of government offices as well as private companies following government rules and regulations. Adoption from abroad doubles the problems.

The following account is a real experience and although it contains more than simply interactions with civil servants or civil regulations, it's worth noting how that these interactions enter in Russia and in different states in the U.S.

In the United States

The first hurdle in adoption is something that natural parents do not have to go through. Theoretically, it answers several needed questions: Are you suitable to have a child? Are you free of offences against a child? Is your home suitable for a child? Do you have enough where-withal to take care of a child?

Unfortunately, the social workers that carry out these home studies go much further than this. There is nothing into which they don't feel they may pry ... rational or not, relevant or not.

This was especially so when a first representative (read 'owner') of one adoption agency appeared. She was a frustrated "grandmother." She wanted continuous ties to the adopted child after it had become our legal child as well as visitation rights for three years. She was also going to prepare outings for the child and determine, in part, whom the child met. She had even planned who would be Father Christmas. We clearly didn't get on and she bowed out with a little push.

Then we found a more objective agency and completed the "Home Study" process. It did indeed delve into every private part of one's life: home, jobs, finances, investments, wealth, parents, relatives, one's childhood, relationships, sex habits, biographies, taxes, friends, neighbors, belongings … have I left anything out? They didn't. The assessor, who was probably more in tune with the old-fashioned brown wood décor of her own home, even suggested that we should redecorate our modern home. The only fortunate thing that stopped questions in one area was that all my older relatives had died and could not be questioned.

This woman had a mission to accomplish but she did it with a prurient interest in other people's relationships. This violation of one's private life is intended, of course, to ensure that the home is a suitable one for the child. Yet nothing of this sort is done when two people, married or not, with money or not, or even with any sort of sanity or not, or even today of the same sex, have a child. Society apparently thinks those conditions are OK, but an "adoption" is a case in which governments and the states can get involved and they do.

All this time, the adopting parents are supplicants rather than applicants. They know full well that if any enemy is created anywhere along the way, that avenue would quickly be closed.

For the home study one has to compile a set of papers: birth certificates, divorce and marriage certificates, tax returns, home deeds, bank records, medical records, certification of, and by, your doctor, police records, felony records, state records and many more. All have different requirements for certification, affirmation, confirmation by a notary public, and apostilling[41]. Furthermore, all require that someone be paid and all have termination dates and, so, might have to be repeated.

Many questions are unreasonable. For example, the agency demanded to know exactly how many square feet my home's lot size was and they wanted proof. Yet I knew that a single woman living in a trailer on a rented lot had been approved for an adoption. Why did the lot size of my single-family suburban dwelling make a difference? Not once were we given a set of criteria to meet. Many seemed to be invented on the fly.

For a foreign adopted child's U.S. immigration certification one has to complete another set of papers, some of which overlapped the previous pile but which, nevertheless, have to be produced a second time, often to different formats. This paperwork goes to a U.S.

---

[41] The Apostille treaty is an international treaty drafted by the Hague Conference on Private International Law. It specifies the modalities through which a document issued in one of the signatory countries can be certified for legal purposes in all the other signatory states. Such a certification is called an **apostille**. It is an international certification comparable to a notarization in domestic law.

Embassy in the foreign country – in this case in Moscow.

Then, jumping ahead, the foreign court (in this case Russian) requires another dossier of documents, which again overlap and extend the previous piles of documents with sometimes even different requirements for confirming and apostilling.

This is a time to hold your breath and control your temper, because there are many clerks along the way who follow procedures without understanding what they are doing. No one for example, during this process knew why documents were apostilled.

Further, I am a writer and a scientific consultant and my wife and myself partner a small company. I choose not to take a salary but to work only for expenses. It benefits our tax position. However, at first, our agency wanted confirmation that I earned no money over and beyond what the tax returns told them. They needed that confirmation by a Certified Public Accountant properly notarized and apostilled. Remember -- the agency is trying to see whether the child could be supported … it was not clear why they required proof that I had no income from this source? There are many other sources that didn't pay me a cent. Should I have them all confirm that they pay me nothing?

But to step back one moment. We lived in Colorado but the agency that has most experience with Russia is in Wyoming, so there were also papers concerning the respective standing of the agencies, interagency agreements, medical practitioners, and various legal requirements from two states involved. We often held our breath as matters crawled along.

After all the forms had been completed and having read 35 hours of infant-care instruction our Colorado Home Study was approved and matters moved to the Wyoming Children's Society agency.

To be honest, these agencies do the best they can within the regulations. That is a standard excuse … "it's the regulation," either of the state, the U.S State Department or the Russian Courts. Not once did I see any attempt to provide agency feedback on some requirements, which were egregious nonsense. They were not into protecting their supplicants.

How much does the process cost?

A lot … of the order of $40,000 in the end with only a small amount returned through tax concessions and then only if the adoption is successful. We were still counting long after the event.

It seems that everyone along the road to adoption has his or her hand out. It is a process that makes one feel uncomfortable. Notary publics need $2 an attestation, municipalities need $3 to $5 for copies of certifications, the police need $50 for each fingerprinting (which are good for only six months) and $40 for each court record search, adoption agencies need up to $3,500 for Home Studies, the U.S. immigration service needs $665 for a form, Russian visa fees for two trips cost a minimum of $1,200, the state agency needed $35 each for attesting to the fact that neither of us had been a child abuser. Applications for everything usually cost $100 a go, and we haven't even reached the adoption placement agency.

Then the fees get large: $3,500 to start the process and $14,900 for successfully identifying a child. Two trips are needed to Russia: one to see the child and one to adopt it legally. The visits, for two, with accommodation, can run to another $15,000 especially since, in some cases, the supplicant parent can be forced to stay for several weeks. In that case loss of earnings enter into the equation.

In the Russian Republic

While in Russia there are further "expectations": interpreters are provided at up to $60 a day, drivers at $55 a day, medical center fees at $100, embassy fees at $335, passport processing at $102, registration fees at $115, a child's visa at $335 and more. Are you tallying the list?

Then there are 'contributions,' not bribes, a 'donation' to the orphanage of $300, shopping for 'one's baby' at $170, and other materials for the orphanage from juice to office paper, a tea party for the workers, to office stationery at another $50. We sign a form to say we will not offer bribes at the same time as we are told that the Russian judge personally expects $350 after each court session.

Did I forget to tip somebody along the way? Did I forget to grease someone's palm?

Most of these people are clerks following regulations and the regulations are their weapons to ensure that contributions are forthcoming. No grease and there may be another regulation, which declares that your application cannot be read this month.

As the agency says, "prices are subject to change without notice and the list may not be inclusive." We found that it was not. An act as remote as one by the Russian Dumas could increase 'expectations.'

This easily adds up to $40,000 even before you consider the child's needs at home … and there is more to come.

The only bright spot on the horizon in our case was that airline prices could be less by not traveling in a holiday period. We were due to travel to Russia in January where temperatures hover around −10 to −20 degrees Centigrade. However, that date changed.

Throughout the initial negotiations the placement agency had spoken of 'Russia' as being composed of Moscow or St. Petersburg and we were shown films of a St. Petersburg orphanage. Then it finally became clear that they dealt primarily with Vladivostok orphanages and not Moscow at all.

Vladivostok is at the end of the Siberian railway on the Sea of Japan. It is less than 50 miles from China and from North Korea. Now, lest this sounds like the ends of the earth … it really isn't. Vladivostok was closer to Denver where we lived than was Moscow. Travel is simply through Incheon, Korea, rather than through Munich, Europe.

There is a hitch however. Even though the adoption could be accomplished in a Russian court in Vladivostok the only way to have the child made a US citizen was at the US embassy in Moscow so our second trip would need both a visit to Vladivostok and to Moscow … a round-the-world episode. The alternative would be a costly Russian courier to carry papers to Moscow while we twiddled our thumbs in Vladivostok. The issue added about another $3,000 to the costs.

An alternative idea of a trip on the Trans-Siberian railway sounded wonderful … it fitted one of our long-term travel ambitions ... but with a strange three-month-old baby? We decided, "No."

Finally after months of waiting, a baby girl was identified in Vladivostok.

We were told was that she had been born in September sometime between the 1st and the 30th so she was two or three months old. There was no other information: no photographs, no name, no orphanage address, no medical history, nothing. The placement clerk refused every request as if we were asking for the world. However she told us that we **had** to be in Vladivostok on January 18th.

Before we could book flights we had to make flight reservations so that they could be approved in Russia. Approved? What did an official need to know more than that we would be arriving by a given flight at a given time? Would our travel plans have been disapproved if we had come at a different hour? None of the organizations' representatives bothered to answer questions.

In fact, flight arrangements were not easy. There are no flights to Vladivostok from Japan. There is one flight a day, some days, from Seoul to Vladivostok by Korean Airlines and that flight is often fully booked with Korean gamblers aiming to lose hard currency at the tables in Vladivostok. Eventually, at a cost of some $5,500 we managed a reservation using United and Korean Airlines for dates exactly a week later than originally required. We waited for four days for approval of the details of how we would fly from Denver to San Francisco to Seoul to get to Vladivostok. It would take one overnight stay in Incheon in both directions

Staying in Vladivostok was yet another doubtful matter. A western hotel with excellent amenities could not be used because they didn't pay 'commission' to the adoption agencies. Commission? It was simply another palm to be greased and the hotel objected. Our placement agency contact was unsympathetic.

However, we knew that there was a little baby girl in Vladivostok that could become ours if we didn't stir the pot too much. The problem is that in this line of business, adoption personnel know that they are dealing with emotional couples, which have usually already gone through every other option. We, like other couples wanted the baby first, so justice and fair dealing took a back seat.

The principal issue was the baby's health and the fetal baby syndrome. It is at the forefront of one's mind. Almost no meaningful medical information is available. The placement clerk was unsympathetic, "It's never available." She was certainly not going to bother to ask on this occasion simply because we needed to know.

In past years it was a regulation that no healthy baby could be adopted from the Soviet Union … it had to be handicapped … so in today's Russia the orphanages are also very vague about health issues and might even make note of health issues that could be nothing although they seem to infer that the baby is really crippled with problems. The parents would not know. Thus, we were advised to take a movie camera to film the baby's responses and then to take the resulting films to specialized doctors (at home) who could evaluate the baby from the film and provide advice.

So ... a new camera was purchased, trial films were made in low light and we were prepared to hope for the best. Our agency contact was vague as to even whether we would be allowed to use a camera even though the agency recommended it.

One problem throughout the process is that information, such as it was, emerged slowly and was never offered freely, even though the clerks must have known what was on every supplicant's minds.

First, we did know of the Russian practice of holding back healthy children for Russian adoption and freeing only sickly children for U.S. adoption. This was supposedly done because the U.S. has more money to cope with serious ailments involving hospitalization. (I wanted to remind everyone that the U.S. might have more money to deal with serious ailments but we didn't.) We were told, wrongly, that was the old system. We found later that it was close to the truth.

Second, we did not know, at the home study stage, that there was a minimum income requirement to qualify.

Third, for the second visitation stage, we did not know that we could use a courier to Moscow instead of traveling around the world and we did not know that the two-week second visit was probably three weeks' long if one didn't qualify for a waiver of a ten-day stay in Vladivostok for 'serious medical issues'. Potential loss of earnings became an issue.

Lastly, and more seriously, we did not know that the Dumas had a bill under consideration to restrict adoptions. The Russian adoption-agency representative knew but he still allowed us to book expensive flights that we might not be able to use. His motivation was the $15,000 that was due on acceptance of a child prospect, nothing more.

I suspect there is much more that we do not know even today.

To illustrate what was told to us by the various contact personnel and what was not:

We knew that there was a baby girl available for adoption 8 time zones away. We knew we would have to make two visits if everything went successfully. We knew that our immediate costs would be approximately $22,000.

Nothing more was known about the baby other than that she was born sometime in September. We did not know for sure that she was Caucasian in that Mongol region. We did not know anything about her health although the orphanage had much of this information. That made it impossible to form a judgment before getting to Vladivostok.

But my wife felt 'pregnant' and wanted to enjoy the feeling that a baby girl was imminent ... and I loved her for that.

Then the Dumas acted. It decreed that no child be released for adoption until it was six-months old, to allow for Russian adoptions of healthy babies. The Russian adoption agency knew that the bill was being discussed but didn't warn anyone before flights were locked in. Later Alexey, the Russian representative, wrote, "We'll have to cancel to Graham-Roos visit" even though the bill before the Dumas must have been on its books months before -- even before we were encouraged to make flight and hotel reservations.

John Graham

Russian holidays last until January 10th and apparently
even though the Dumas could act, the Russian
adoption people couldn't get any information before
January 10th. Had the baby girl been released from the
rolls before the Dumas decision? Had she slipped
under the wire of new regulations? Do we cancel
flights? Do we not? Answers were simply not
forthcoming.

Then another phone call: No, she had not slipped
under the regulatory wire. Our trip had to be cancelled
and everything was put on hold. Fortunately, our
cancellation meant simply additional work and some
cancellation fees. However, we were also told that one
set of prospective U.S. parents had been allowed to
travel. On January 11th they were sent home without
even seeing a child. They had to eat the expenses of
about $5,000 for that useless trip.

Our Wyoming agency staff always operated with the
best of intentions and seemed to be as much perplexed
as anyone else with what was happening.
Unfortunately, they were nice people, all women, and
they were not given to questioning what was
happening or even demanding that their Russian
representatives do the job they were being paid
generously to do. Unlike us, they suffered fools and
dishonest behavior gladly and passed on quite useless
information. They went home at 5:00 p.m. content
that they had done their jobs.

The next news was that the Vladivostok Health
department had added another month to the Dumas
requirement of the child being a full six months old
before it could be referred for adoption. A March trip
became April and then May in successive e-mails and
the 'child' got older.

This additional delay now put possible visits into the part of the year in which Russians go on vacation again –in early May or in June. The placement agency clerk suggested that the solution might be to take all the official paperwork over on the first trip to get that processed early even though we might elect not to take the referral child or return for a second trip. I suspect the idea that it might result in dollars-in-hand occurred to the Russians ... it would be very difficult to refund thousands of U.S. dollars from Vladivostok if the referred child was not of one's choice.

Furthermore, U.S. official papers also had termination dates and since many had been prepared twelve months ago we had to do an immediate search to find out which had to be renewed ... at more cost of course.

Dreams

The acquisition of a baby is supposed to be a wonderful time ... a happy time ... like a wedding. It was to be 'a birth'. Yet, our dreams didn't reflect this, instead they reflect the overwhelmingly bureaucratic 'process', the unresponsiveness of clerks, and our fears.

The father-to-be dreams

I was searching through the grey deserted streets, peering up at dirty signs, and matching them against the hand-drawn map my Mother had given me, when I met a friend. He agreed to come with me because the museum didn't seem to be far away.

Abolskaya. Ah! I remember that on the map. Yes, there. Turn right into Stelnikov Place and across. There's the museum.

John Graham

*We ran across the square beneath dark
leafless limbs and chattered up the steps to the
door. Inside there is a desk with a very old
man keeping watch.*

*"Oh no!" he said, "There are no children's
tickets here. You need the Trek museum on
Slovskaya." He gives muttered instructions
while I try to follow the route on my map.*

*We thanked him and we ran down across the
square again and out along a broad avenue,
then right, and right again and left into
another avenue. We crossed two squares, and
then down a long street with trees from which
last year's growth had been cut. They were
dark and weird under the day's clouds.*

*As we got closer, there was no one around to
ask for directions, the place was empty, but
then all of a sudden, there it was: the Trek
museum, solid against the sky. Again we ran
up the steps and here there was another
reception desk. This time a very tall guardian
in a brown uniform stood behind it. When he
heard my request, he leant far down across his
desk and thrust his face into mine.*

*"We don't give free entry tickets here. You
must go to the office on Kramnik Street.*

*We started off again with new instructions,
street after street of apartments and then solid
offices, until we reached Kramnik Street.
There it was, number 2320. We pushed open
the old brown doors and trudged up two
flights of stairs to the office for Museum
Tickets.*

I knocked and we went in. There was a bell on a counter. I rang it and the sound echoed into the distance down empty halls

There was a long pause and just as I had been about to ring the bell again, the door behind the counter opened and a woman came in brushing her hair back and adjusting her dress. There was a sound of a man's laughter behind her.

When she had found and lit a cigarette, I made my request for children's free entry to the Trek Museum.

She grimaced and said, "Yes, this is the office, but I am too busy to fill out forms for you today. Come back tomorrow and don't forget to bring back a letter from your mother to say how old you are. You don't look under ten to me. If the office is closed tomorrow, then come back the next day."

Then I awoke and discovered that I had been dreaming about the U.S. adoption process.

It was no different for either of us. We simply had different fears.

The mother–to-be dreams

I was in the orphanage.

There were eight white iron cribs in an equally white room. The room had big windows with big curtains that didn't seem to have closed or opened in years. Our baby was sitting in front of us on a little thin carpet.

The caretaker in the room suddenly came over and picked up the baby. Our time to spend with the child was at an end.

We left the orphanage and as I walked out, I realized that I had forgotten to memorize her face. I panicked because now I wouldn't be able to recognize her when I saw her during our second trip, the one when we might take her home. I also realized that we hadn't taken a photo of her so I had nothing to look at home or anything to recognize her face by.

Then I saw a newspaper article about a study that showed that people who had visited Vladivostok were getting cancer.

... and I woke up.

So, the process continued.

My wife was very brave during these days. She complained of the problems and of the people we dealt with, of course, but there were no tears.

Adopting is not the happy occasion that it should be.

Two trips were involved and we were due to make the first in January. The flights and hotel bookings were all set.

Because of the delays decreed by the Dumas and the additional delay added by the Vladivostok Health Ministry, the little girl who had been referred to us had grown from three to six to nine to ten months old. We had to screw with our minds to keep up with the changes. Looking in children's shops my wife had to keep revising her shopping list … from that for a helpless baby to a child who could almost walk.

Then all the arrangements, flights and hotels, had to be cancelled again. Again the official contact had not warned us that this might happen.

While January had been affected by mandatory Russian government end-of-year vacations, we were now seemingly beginning to encroach upon the period of their mandatory summer vacations. Civil servants love their vacations. So the adoption agencies arranged the first trip to do some of the things that the second trip would have done – at extra and irrecoverable cost, of course.

Now, for the first time, we found that instead of traveling on two successive and expensive tourist visas we were able to travel on one 3-month business visa that allowed two trips. I had asked before why this wasn't possible since I had been to Russia before and I was told that it simply wasn't. Now it apparently was. The agency clerks had simply never bothered to ask.

We were also asked to make a tentative decision about the baby during the first trip and perhaps attend court to settle the adoption even though the interval between the two trips had been designed to get medical advice based on first-trip knowledge. We are told that the 'decision' before the court was revocable but the idea of reneging on an international court decision didn't seem the safest thing to do. It all added up to more pressure.

A positive decision on this first trip would also incur an immediate payment of $14,900 to the Russian organization so "Alexey" was obviously keen on making that happen. The money would be quickly pocketed away. "Alexey" (no surname) was a facilitator operating out of Moscow reporting to someone in Pennsylvania so it is not clear how these funds were distributed or whether they could ever be refunded. It was almost certain that a payment of this kind was not 'revocable.'

We were also asked to take a laminated picture of ourselves to hang on the baby's crib while we were away between visits. That seemed to be an even bigger commitment and something that a baby, who could be rejected, didn't need … especially if orphanage staff emphasized that these two people in the picture were to be "Mama and Dada."

This was called 'extending the family'. It is part of the pressure placed on the family seeking an adoption. Orphanage staffs want to see babies moved since more were arriving every day.

Two matters remained to be completed. First, we needed personal medical examinations, again, with documentation for the court. That meant carefully arranged diagnoses on the doctor's stationary, attested by us, and then apostilled in Wyoming together with copies of the doctor's medical qualifications also attested and apostilled. Amazingly these requirements didn't seem to worry our doctor except that his certification expired very quickly after our examinations and before any Russian court dates. This now required that yet another copy of his new certification to be attested and apostilled. Indeed, the attestations, certifications, apostillings, and so forth were clearly more important to the staff of the agency than the results of the health examination. We could have been mentally insane and inflicted with AIDS as long as the paperwork was in order.

We could imagine the Vladivostok judge admiring the various seals applied by notary publics and state officials without much idea of what the English text said. Translations by the Russian agency would certainly affirm us to be healthy. Alternatively, the judge might not even see the paperwork.

The orphanage then increased their 'voluntary' contribution request by $200 because the lack of anxious parents-to-be during the Dumas-declared delay had made them short of funds. We were due to make good the shortfall.

Each time we questioned financial commitments the agency contact would ask, "You do want a baby, don't you?"

The first-trip costs were now said to be:

Use of a car for 6 days, $330

Use of an interpreter for 6 days, $330

"Gift" to orphanage, $500

Purchase of 30-day supply of food for child, $170

Purchase of formula, diapers, wet wipes, balmex, & stationery gifts for the orphanage, $50

Total   **$1,380**

We were asked to carry between $2,500 and $4,000 in new un-creased U.S. bills even though hotels and many meals would be paid for by credit card. I decided on $2,500 expecting to bring a lot back for the second trip.

However, the problem was now to obtain un-creased U.S. bills that the Russian bank could trust. Our "full-service" U.S. bank said that such bills would have to be specially ordered and they didn't know whether it was possible with only a week's notice.

Later, the purchase of foods and consumable supplies increased to $402 and the U.S. Consulate in Vladivostok charged us $50 each for notary affirmations so the ancillary bill became $1,662

Time passes. Sometimes it didn't seem to but eventually our flight reservations were remade, we were told the local representatives would make the hotel reservations, and May 7th approached. We were told that someone would meet us at Vladivostok airport with our names written on a card. Other than the information I had downloaded for the hotel from the Internet we were given neither local phone numbers nor the name of the orphanage.

We decided to reserve the hotel ourselves and to reject the local recommendation. That turned out to be wise for the recommendation had been for the casino hotel where hard currency could be lost easily and the noise never ceased.

My wife and I also elected to fly United Airlines to Seoul, overnight there and continue on Korean Air the next day. Other families took the children's society's advice and flew the whole way on Korean Air. They found themselves spending five hours in Incheon airport from 5:00 a.m. to 10:00 a.m. waiting for the connection. They were exhausted on arrival at Vladivostok. The problem here was that the society's representative had no experience with international travel and simply gave advice as though the journey was a bus ride down the road.

Only Korean, Aeroflot, and Vladivostok-Air serve Vladivostok. It has a single departure lounge but entering and exiting travelers go through immigration twice in each direction. Don't ask why! It was a regulation and we were now enured to regulations.

On Monday, the person holding a card with our names at the airport told us that nothing would happen that day apart from our being taken to the hotel, and, moreover, nothing would happen the next day. Thus, we could only visit the orphanage on Wednesday afternoon, two days later than expected. Bear in mind that the orphanage expected a life-changing decision before we left Vladivostok on Saturday morning.

Why the delay? Monday was an annual Russian national holiday celebrating the Soviet victory over the Nazis 60 years before. It was so important that American President Bush attended celebrations in Moscow. It was so important that Tuesday would also be a national holiday to recover from the excesses of Monday. It was apparently so important in Russia that Alexey had, nevertheless, arranged for five American families to come to Vladivostok that week, knowing that they would not be able to visit the orphanage and that their opportunity to see the prospective children was cut in half. My hatred for Alexey was growing.

The adoption representative took us to our hotel on Monday afternoon and arranged for transport to the Ministry of Education on Wednesday. The U.S. Consulate would have to be visited on Thursday to complete a Power of Attorney and Friday morning would be spent buying gifts for the orphanage.

Saturday we would leave. However, none of this was clear to us before arriving at Vladivostok airport ... we expected to spend four days getting acquainted with a strange child. Now it might only be a few hours. In the end it amounted to about 4 hours.

However, the delay gave ample time for us to see Vladivostok ... walking its hills and exploring a beautifully located but unkempt and seedy city. The day was fine and sunny and we enjoyed tourist exploration. Having done some research on the Internet we visited the university, two art galleries, some small shops, and restaurants for local food. It was a fine day and very pleasurable if we had not come 8,000 miles to do something else.

On the Wednesday, we were taken by car to the Ministry of Education, an office block behind other office blocks. At the elevator our local adoption facilitator, Ms. Yelena Chemeriova, went ahead to clear the way. She came back to announce that we couldn't be seen because the computers were down. We were to come back in an hour after papers had been completed by hand.

In an hour we were told things were not complete and we should wait for another 20 minutes. After twenty minutes we were told that the civil servant who had to sign the papers had attended a meeting and would not be coming back for the rest of the day. Apparently, he was not concerned about visitors from thousands of miles away with very little time. We should come again tomorrow. We were driven back to the hotel and spent another half-day sightseeing. By now the weather had turned wet and our mood was black.

On the Thursday, we returned to the Ministry of Education and lined up in a corridor. Eventually, one couple after another was seen by a clerk and asked the same questions we had been asked by every official clerk before and which we had answered in papers that had been notarized, certified, apostilled and translated months before. This was bureaucratic nonsense.

Stay calm.

Here we also found that the expert, Alexey in Moscow, having demanded proof of my wife's passport renewal weeks before had not bothered to tell the authorities. This lapse delayed us three times in the next two days. Fortunately, I had several Xerox copies of both passports with me and could prove the changes fairly quickly.

After the Ministry of Education we were finally taken to the orphanage.

It was on the edge of town … two buildings joined by an enclosed and elevated walkway. One building was a children's hospital and one was the orphanage. We would spend all our time in the enclosed walkway. It had been converted into a long room full of cribs, toys, and plants.

We arrived in torrential rain … not a good omen. Entry was through a rear steel door. Inside, we were asked to put on overshoes … but then it was found that they had run out of overshoes. "You will have to buy some tomorrow."

We met the manager of the orphanage, and, briefly, a Director, who ran both buildings. Neither of the meetings produced information. Then we were asked to wait at the entrance to the walkway.

My wife and I were to be the first of the five couples to receive a child.

Very shortly, a lady in a white gown brought in a small child in a yellow outfit, which she laid in my wife's arms. The other couples gathered around and "oohed" and "aahed" at the first sign that something was happening. Ms. Chemeriova appeared and asked us, "Do you love your baby?"

The nameless baby girl appeared to be the age we had been expecting, just under a year. She had a yellow terry-towel outfit with a white cap. Her eyes were a beautiful blue set above a wide-open mouth between chubby cheeks. She looked a Soviet Russian and a total stranger. However, we answered Ms. Chemeriova's question with a "Yes."

How else could you answer the question? There was no privacy and we had not met the baby although we had spent 18 months, $20,000 and traveled 8,000 miles for this moment. Five hours later, back in our hotel, we found that the baby had stirred nothing in either of our minds but doubt. 'Love' was not even an issue.

The other four couples all received their babies in the same atmosphere while we took ours down the hall to 'bond,' as our American agency clerk had said we should.

The next couple of hours passed quickly while we played with the babies and fed them at lunchtime. Ours was the oldest and by far the largest, but her mouth remained gaping open, so much so that the other couples noticed it. Without being cruel, she looked simple.

During the day, while my wife was feeding the 'baba' we were taken to meet the doctor, Dr. Irina.

She gave us a sheet of medical history and explained it to us. She also told us that we couldn't keep it nor take a copy.

The baby, whose name was Victoria Vladimirovna Mysova, had been born almost nine months before. She was the third child of her 31-year-old single smoking mother and had been born at home without prenatal care. During the birth she had suffered a dislocated hip, had suffered early pneumonia of a moderate degree of gravity and respiratory failure of the 2nd degree. In addition she had cerebral ischemia of the 2nd degree, had a mild case of anemia and she had rickets. She was five-months delayed in normal child development, in just nine months.

Dr. Irina said none of these things mattered. But my wife and I were separately making our own silent diagnoses. We had been warned to expect some documented problems because in the past no child could be adopted from outside Russia without being disabled. The orphanages were said to play up minor problems out of habit. However, in accepting a child who would live with us for the rest of our lives no existing problem was minor.

We knew also that the Russian authorities were of the opinion that America was rich and could afford to give a child medical attention that was not possible in their own country. However, we were not rich and we could not afford to have a child that needed either medical or psychiatric therapies. This list of problems, which had been visited upon poor Victoria, was not reassuring. My wife particularly worried about the respiratory failure while I worried about the gaping mouth and cerebral ischemia.

Suddenly, my wife who was still feeding the child was invited to change the baby's napkin even though she didn't need it. It was an elementary test of motherly competence and I was glad that the doctor had not asked me.

However, Victoria's lower limbs, thus revealed, were enormous and ugly. I had felt her fat thighs through her clothes and had wondered. Now I saw that her limbs were creased in a very unnatural way and coupled with her gaping mouth, I thought that I saw my cousin … a retarded child. The cerebral ischemia and respiratory failure fitted.

"Do you love your baby?"

Back with the other parents who also had interviews with the doctor, the mood varied from one couple who now called their child by an American name and addressed each other as "Mummy" and "Daddy," to another couple who visualized the need for an immediate hernia operation, and still another who wondered why the baby's legs would not bend.

At the end of the afternoon we were driven silently back to our hotel. We sat together and my wife, the most loving of individuals, suddenly said that she had felt no connection with Victoria. There was no spark of recognition that this might be our child. I had not said anything to this point, but I too had felt nothing for Victoria but sympathy while we had played together and I was very worried about the information that told me to expect a retarded child. We, separately and together, decided there and then that Victoria was not our child.

We also decided not to tell anyone straight away even though it would have saved us nearly two thousand dollars in fees and 'gifts.' The orphanage at least deserved those contributions. Furthermore, we felt that it was necessary to meet with Victoria for a little longer than three hours. Something might click.

On the Friday, we were taken to shops to buy goods for the orphanage. We bought those plastic overshoes as well as copier paper and toner for the orphanage office. Then we were all taken to a children's store, nominally to buy supplies for our child in the two months before we could return to claim her. Poor Victoria was fat enough already and the amount we were asked to buy would have destroyed her. We were simply asked to buy food, consumable supplies, and toys for the orphanage under the guise of "our baby."

Our shopping cart cost over $450, instead of the expected $170, and despite being told that we could use credit cards, the credit-card machine was 'out-of-order'. We had to pay in U.S. dollars. Our translator, a pleasant University student named Marina, explained with a shrug that the machine was always out of order in the presence of Americans who had been told to bring U.S. dollars.

On returning to the orphanage we were reminded that the authorities also expected a Humanitarian Aid contribution, which had just risen by two hundred dollars to $500. This was also payable in clean un-creased U.S. dollars.

Receipts that the U.S. IRS might need were hard to come by ... probably because dealing in U.S. dollars is illegal. However, after some persuasion the shop and the orphanage did provide receipts for the equivalent number of rubles. The adoption agency representative, Ms. Chemeriova, was a different matter. She wanted to settle our bill at the airport when our priority would be to board a plane on time. Finally, I settled a couple of hours earlier and she was dismayed that I paid $550 for translators and drivers in U.S. dollars with the final $50 in rubles at a generous exchange rate. Of course, I received no receipt.

"Do you love your baby?"

By now, the other couples were calling their referral babies by American names and they had been clad in American clothes. However, we thought of ours only as Victoria. I had, at first, been pleased that her second patronymic name celebrated her father Vladimir ... at least they knew her father, I thought. However, since a patronymic is mandatory in Russia, we were told that 'Vladimir' probably only existed in a clerical imagination.

We hadn't changed our mind about the referral on the final evening and even went along to meet Victoria again on Saturday morning before we all left for the return flights. We wanted the orphanage to get the benefit of our visit, and we did not want to engage in the poorly understood but fervent persuasion that might have resulted from the Russians if we had said, "No" early.

On the first morning back in the United States, I phoned our Adoption agency, and in response to the representative's enthusiastic greeting said that the trip had been a good one but that we had decided to refuse the referral.

"What?"

"We have decided to refuse the baby that was offered. Neither my wife nor I felt any connection and there was simply too much doubt about her health for us to accept her."

There was silence. Perhaps no one had ever refused a baby before despite the process allowing that possibility. Certainly, our agency worker was astounded. She had read too much into our noncommittal phone conversations during the prior week. The gung-ho atmosphere of acceptance had been shattered in her mind.

From that point on, she went cold. The agency went cold. There was no suggestion of other possibilities, instead my wife had to ask. Apparently, in reality one had to accept whatever was offered even though it might be bad for the baby as well as the prospective family.

During the prior week I had asked the agency whether any previous adoptee had some of the same difficulties to which Victoria had suffered. The answer was "Yes, we have a little boy in the Jackson Hole area and he is now three. He is fine. He can now recognize that when the car keys are rattled on the kitchen table they are going out in the truck." At first that sounded reassuring until my wife pointed out that a dog can learn the same response much earlier. We would have been more impressed with a sign of independent thought before three.

This is a letter we received from our adoption agency a week or so after our refusal of Victoria:

To repeat what we said in our earlier email, Vladivostok refuses to send photos, medical information and video to families prior to seeing the child and if you remember, Vladivostok was the only region without an age restriction.

As we see it, the only option for you is to repeat the process and travel for another first trip to Vladivostok for another blind referral of a baby girl and travel a second trip for the court.

We have received your initial refusal letter and it is being apostilled at the Secretary of State in Denver. It will be sent to Russia when we receive it back from Denver.

Let us know if you wish to proceed with Vlad (ivostok).

We were told that no Russian city (other than Vladivostok) was willing to work with parents, which included an older husband. Two lesbians or a single woman would be acceptable. This was not an option for us since at that time my wife was Belgian while I am an American citizen. I couldn't even 'divorce' her to allow her to adopt alone.

Furthermore, we were told that not one Russian orphanage would send photographs or medical reports ahead of a visit. This we now understood because once there, whatever the child's health and whatever the child's background, the pressure to accept the referral is almost overwhelming. "Do you love your baby?" That pressure could not be exerted remotely if one was in greater possession of the facts. In this the local agency were as much at fault as those in Russia.

We then wondered whether a more specific description of the child from our side would help and I asked whether it would be possible for the U.S. Consulate's doctor to see the child before we traveled. After all both the Ministry of Education and the Orphanage in Vladivostok knew us now.

The response?

None.

Moreover, from the tone of the agency's words, it was clear that the agency had never asked for options. They are not willing to push the envelope while there are a sufficient number of desperate couples willing to do anything for any baby under existing regulations.

The episode ... traveling to Vladivostok with a great deal of hope and expectation ... being faced with a decision that the agency had expected not to be a decision ... and, returning with much greater knowledge of the process, transformed my wife from a person with hope for the future to one facing the grim reality that a child might never happen.

We both despair of the adoption process and the servants who administer it. It was geared to satisfy desperate couples within existing unquestioned regulations. Abroad (at least in Russia) it was geared to use desperate couples to solve a national orphan problem. In between, representatives who have become entrepreneurs make the most of the regulations to make a rich living. A change of the regulations would help no one except the adopting couples. Perhaps this is too skeptical but probably not.

I can only imagine the turmoil that my wife went through. No civil servant or agency representative in the adoption process or in all the training prepared us for the trauma of having to give a refusal. I saw only the external signs of my wife's having to explain to friends and loved ones that her hopes had been dashed and she had virtually suffered a 'miscarriage.' This time it was worse because we had been offered Victoria and we had both made the rejection decision. On the surface, that makes one feel guilty and it was impossible not to think of what might come of Victoria. Perhaps she will gain parents more capable of keeping a handicapped child.

The Wyoming adoption agency viewed our photographs and film and wrote that:

"We shared the video with a registered nurse practitioner with several years of experience evaluating kids adopted internationally. All of us were impressed with Victoria and thought she looked like a very nice baby."

Unfortunately, "nice" is not sufficient medical diagnosis to take on a baby with significant recorded defects that could turn one's lives into that of constant-care givers, especially when those calling her a 'nice baby' were unwilling to review the medical history that I offered to them.

Our Wyoming agency was not deficient by agency standards. They did their best but were willing to be 'taken' in by Russian rules and regulations. It would benefit the agency to have some men involved in the work who then might be less forgiving of Russian entrepreneurial duplicity.

It would have been nice to be prepared by the agency for a refusal. Unfortunately, despite my advice to the contrary, they also wanted to "offer" Victoria to another couple and they were willing to use our photographs to show that she looked a 'nice' baby. However, when I offered to send a copy of her medical report that I had noted down they didn't want it. It would perhaps have revealed too much to the next anxious set of 'parents to be.' In this way, the Wyoming agency and its representatives were as duplicitous and guilty as anyone in the process.

After two weeks at home, my wife said that she had come to the conclusion that she could not go through a Russian visitation again. Of the five children that we had seen, she could, on the surface, have been content with two even though we had not seen their medical history. Those odds were simply not good enough so she had given up on the adoption process.

Costs were finally $15,971.31 in 2005 dollars. By our refusal of Victoria the Russian adoption agency contacts immediately suffered a minimum loss of another $20,000 so their concern that the baby should be adopted, whatever her state of health, was understandable.

The public servants in Vladivostok were total automatons. Their unsmiling attitude reflected that they were merely filling the hours before quitting time. Only one was pleasant and helpful: Marina, a student from the University who was acting as our interpreter. Of course, she wasn't a permanent agency employee and so hadn't yet been subdued into the common unthinking mold. She recognized our concerns and told us the truth. The credit card machine was always out of order if Americans with dollars were present.

In contrast, Ms. Chemeriova was plainly in it for the money, especially when that money was in clean U.S. dollars. Her most intense desire was that referrals be accepted so that she would get her cut. Before that she extracted as many of the dollars carried by prospective parents as was possible. Despite her smile and busy manner, she was a cold grasping person.

From this tale you can see the range of civil servants and representatives involved. Some simply filled in the hours of their day with no thought of whom they were dealing with or what their concerns might be.

The Russian public servants were a little colder than those in the U.S.A. but that could simply have seemed so because of the difference in language and some of the paranoia that Americans still feel about Russia.

Importing a car

In another complex real example, the characters are all public servants representing a multitude of government agencies but for two clerks of the moving firm. This example is one of unthinking inefficiency. A very similar experience, though not quite as excruciating, appears on the Internet as advice for expats in Belgium.[42]

This example of bureaucratic inefficiency took 27 months from August 2009 to November 2011.

It is possible that having a car to which you have become attached, you might like, on emigration, to take it with you. You might be the sole owner; it might have the right engine; the right accessories and the right leather seats to make it yours. Mine was a 3006 BMW 330i. I thought it should not be a problem to ship in the same container as my furniture, home computer equipment, valuables and clothes.

Ho, ho! Was I naïve!

First, your shipping company (Allied in this case) will give you no inkling of the problem(s) you are about to encounter. It seems that they actually do not know … or care. At best, they require that the car's title be stamped that it is acceptable to be exported, i.e. that no

---

[42] Morris Fraser,
http://www.expatica.com/be/essentials_moving_to
/essentials/importing-your-car-to-belgium-38561.html

taxes remain to be paid on it. Then they will willingly ship it out of the country (here the U.S.A.).

Second, the receiving company (also Allied) has no interest in your needs other than to get the car out of their storage space. Unsympathetic clerks provide the interface with the company. They start by requiring that, in addition to paperwork, a bunch of money be handed over to cover any possible duty that Customs might charge. When one refuses, one is placed at the bottom of the priority list of dealing with Customs. The clerk only provides the requirements of foreign customs when she has to deal with them. She deals with them in the easiest way for her and does not try to find out your needs.

Moreover, it appears that the clerk will never contact the custom's authorities to expedite matters unless she is herself first 'expedited'. Often, the one I dealt with would not answer the phone when she recognized my number.

This is based on a couple of experiences but it could well be a general conclusion.

In addition to shipment papers, U.S. registration papers, proof of U.S. insurance to the moment of shipping, transit insurance, copies of your passport, a residence certificate in Belgium, even more are required. There are some difficult papers. For example, Belgian Customs requires that the shipper had resided in the original country for a year before shipment. This is interpreted as the owner having to provide a copy of all utility bills for the past year ... despite not having been warned of this by the shipper and ... despite the fact that such bills do not show one has lived in a country for any time at all. Anyone living anywhere can pay utility bills. On the other hand, sworn and notarized testimony of a neighbor who saw one every day of the year and knew that one lived next door was apparently insufficient proof. The clerk has been told to obtain one thing and was not paid to consider alternatives. She certainly wasn't going to go out of her way and ask the authorities whether the alternative proof was acceptable.

The real problem is that without Customs clearance, one can't proceed to the next steps of gaining a 'Certificate of Safety Compliance,' and then of registering the car and of getting plates. Without that certificate and those plates, one cannot insure the car, which is required by law before one can drive. However, the applicant has to drive to various offices in a number of cities to acquire the necessary documentation even though he can't legally drive without insurance. Catch 22! He is literally forced to drive illegally to become legal. No insurance company in Belgium or the U.S. would insure the car for a month or two to cover this travel. Fortunately, at the start of this episode the police only gave the U.S. license plate passing notice.

Furthermore, no government servant in the process of importing a car is particularly interested in telling you what one needs to complete the process. The website at the Belgian Embassy in Washington is worse than useless. Furthermore, no one mentions the next increment of cost until the last possible moment.

In this case, five months after arrival of the car in the foreign country, clerks in two shipping companies (in Denver and Brussels), two municipal offices (Hassalt and Hoogstraten), three BMW establishments (Oostmalle, Hoogstraten and Munich), two insurance offices (Denver and Hoogstraten), two technical testing stations (Oostmalle and Deurne) and customs offices in four different cities, (Zaventem, Antwerp, Hassalt and Meer) were all involved. They virtually all had only the responsibility of stamping the last piece of paper obtained in the previous office. Not one attempted to tell one exactly what was needed. There was always something more. However, at any point one could be sent back to correct a prior piece of paper or to start all over again because as one clerk said, "This has been done in the wrong order, you have to come to me first and do things again." It was the modern equivalent of a child's 'Snakes and Ladders'.

Each office clerk scored D- in efficiency at best. Two were better and merited a B. However, the Ministry of Transport in Brussels scored a record low ... there must be a ranking below F. This was due to one minor clerk who neither liked cars from America nor being overseen by an Ombudsman.[43]

There have been bright spots in the process ... these were when each 'competent' authority passed you on to the next. Unfortunately, the moment of elation was only momentary for the phone numbers that were offered for the next step were often out of date, and the clerks in the next office returned phone calls no better than the previous ones and still had little interest in you or your car.

However, the last of four Customs offices finally told me that one could to deal with a 'Customs Expediter' ... a private company that could complete forms using your information and who knew custom's officials

---

[43] The person was Kevin Schulmeister.

personally so that they could pass on cash and get the forms accepted. This was news! The Belgian customs' officer saw neither the humour nor the shame, in having a private company, from across the border in the Netherlands, established purely to complete forms for him and to persuade him to read the forms or at least stamp them as accepted. The payment to the expediter of course also paid the customs' officer. Bribes have a wonderful effect on government servants.

It would have helped if the original importer could have identified an import expediter from the start and explained that palms had to be greased.

Nevertheless, the private company was a relief. Unlike government clerks they had to earn their salary by doing something. They phoned the day they said that they would and dedicated time to get me through the final customs' procedures within four days that included a weekend. They provided information and did their job competently. That was remarkable considering the hassle of the prior four months.

However, that still left two steps … to get a Certificate of Safety Compliance and plates for the car. These steps needed visits to at least three other government offices. One of which took four visits to get satisfaction.

A safety kit was needed … it had four parts: a first-aid kit that was sufficient to bandage a child's hand but not to deal with an accident victim; a visibility vest and a visibility triangle, both of which would have been appropriate when cars traveled a lot slower than they do today; and a fire extinguisher that experts recommended should never be used since it was insufficient for a modern car. However, the four items costing $50 were equivalent to another paper checked-off.

The 'Chef 'at the Technical Testing Center for the Certificate of Compliance was actually helpful. He did things on time and explained, in English, what hurdles had to be overcome. The center tested all manner of things including emissions, doors and hoods, tire tread, brakes, springs, steering, lights and even the diameter of the steering wheel. At the end of testing I was told that there were four 'safety' deficiencies. Since the car was an almost new very low-mileage BMW that was a surprise. The first 'safety' deficiency was that I needed a certificate of the town in which I was residing confirming that I was a resident and that I had come from somewhere else; the second 'safety' deficiency was that I needed a letter from BMW confirming that the engine was what was described in the manual; the third required a rear fog light operated by a switch on the dashboard; and the fourth was that my Xenon lights needed external washers for the light covers. The last requirement threatened to cost several thousand dollars since it potentially included a new front bumper for the car, two additional motors, two pumps plus associated controls. The 'chef' recommended that I apply to the Ministry of Finance (Transport Division) for a waiver.

The addition of a rear fog light ... or at least the addition of a switch on the dash and change of the electronics to a rear light was simplicity as long as one didn't mind parting with 370€.

Then the local BMW dealer refused to confirm that the engine was what it was and referred the question to BMW Munich. They in turn refused to certify the engine since the car came from the USA even though it had been made in Munich and everything matched the original manual. Thus, in desperation, the owner typed a copy of the specifications page from the Car Manual, signed it and presented the page to the safety testing station. It was accepted as one of the 'safety' requirements, despite the actual Manual having been earlier refused as evidence.

Of course, the Ministry of Finance (Transport Division) still had to reply to the waiver request. Phone calls are shuffled through a menu and redirections were made to clerks who were known to be on leave. Finally, the single voice that could be contacted said that no direct phone numbers could be revealed and that it would take three weeks to read an e-mail and redirect it to an officer, who would than take three to five weeks to answer 'yes' or 'no' to the request for a waiver.

It had now been six months since the car arrived in the country and this was apparently still well ahead of the usual experience. One person said that it had taken him 9 months to import a Canadian car and another admitted to 12 months to import a Japanese car. Another expediter was throwing up his arms in despair in trying to import a car from Germany … just a few miles away.

The Ministry of Finance (Transport Division) eventually responded: "We can make no exceptions. The vehicle must comply with technical requirements." Remember, that these official pronouncements are made by an anonymous clerk fulfilling hours until 4:30 p.m. signals the time for preparation to leave for the day.

However, fortunately, it was realized that because of e-mails the ministry might have made a mistake of ignoring the details of the owner that had been provided and had judged the car to be a commercial vehicle. That proved to be the case and finally a waiver was forthcoming … in the government's own sweet time.

The ministry clerk[44] verbally agreed to a waiver … we had a moment of euphoria until I found that the clerk had lied through his teeth. Nothing then happened until we approached the Federal Government's Ombudsman. Then, we found that there was no waiver and nothing had been done … papers had presumably been filed. However, the Ombudsman managed to get the clerk to correct the ownership of the vehicle in the records and respond to an enquiry from the technical testing station.

Then the police appeared … a little Nazi on the sidewalk declared that he would confiscate the car if it was driven. On being told the difficulties, he response was that it was not his problem. It was the standard response of a minor clerk.

Changes were made for the headlight covers to be washed if the Xenon headlights were used in pouring rain. That cost almost a thousand euro and did nothing for the safety of the car. Fortunately, the Federal Technical Testing station, from which good service had been given, agreed that an invoice from BMW for the changes and photographs of the washer working would satisfy them by e-mail. Not having to produce the car all the time for one agency, when it was

---

[44] Ibid.

forbidden to drive it by another, helped.

However, another hurdle appeared. At the last moment one more report was needed for a US imported vehicle … a U.S. CarFax.com report. The report was available on the basis of VIN number from the Internet and the Ministry of Finance (Transport Division) could also have got the report directly. It cost $34.95. The Technical Testing Station then confirmed that all Ministry requirements had been met.

It was apparent that the clerk involved[45] did not like American cars and the requirement for an unofficial CarFax report was a complete invention. Schulmeister was infamous to other car importers. So when the CarFax report came within hours he maliciously did something far worse. Stay tuned.

Then came the wait for the Ministry of Finance (Transport Division) to stamp 'approved' on everything, to collect their fee for months of delay, and then to send me back a form for me to take to the Technical Testing Station for confirmation. You cannot miss this sequence: A sends stuff to B who sends it back and ignores C (the applicant). A tells the applicant to comply with some requirements and send them back to A for them to send to B for B to send to C (the applicant) so that he can take them back to A and have them stamped. The total costs for this rigmarole approaches €2,000 and, all the time, the pristine car is unusable.

Then, out of the blue, came another letter from another branch of the Ministry of Finance (Tax Division), threatening me with a fine of €250.00 as well as

---

[45] Ibid.

payment of taxes 'since my car had been available to drive from the day it landed, a year before'. The taxes added to € 3,674.06. The letter required that I attest within 20 days whether the car had been taken to another country, sold, or was in one's possession and still not registered. In the latter case, the Ministry demanded to know why.

Ministries do not attempt to research a case even within their own Ministry. In this case, a phone call from the Tax Division to the Transport Division of the same Ministry, with a VIN number, would have told them that the case was still being sat on and the vehicle was not registered.

However, I was pleased to tell the tax clerk that Belgian Customs had held things up for 5 months and that the Ministry of Finance (Transport division), had held it up for another 4 months (and counting) and that I would tell her the date when it really was available to drive and she could assess taxes from then, since, of course, road taxes did not apply prior to that.

Then came a letter from the Ministry of Finance (Transport Division)[46] declaring in effect, "Wow! This is an American car and where were the foreign papers? The application had been made in the wrong order and the process should start over again."

However, it was not an American car, it was now a Belgian car owned by a Belgian resident who had a residency certificate and the final customs import papers to show that the car had been imported. After four months, this sort of inanity seemed to point

---

[46] Ibid.

towards vindictiveness … perhaps in retaliation for knowing that a Federal Ombudsman was working on the issue.

The Ombudsman was called in again and he managed to do his thing. Schulmeister admitted that actually all was in order and he promised to pass the file along. It took him four days to do that but the recipient immediately sent me an invoice for this impressive efficiency, which was paid in 15 minutes. Finally, a magnificent stamped and signed form Ministry letter arrived and I was free to complete my safety compliance certification. That took another 40-mile drive. The safety testers completed everything but then told me that the Ministry letter had a significant error in it … it declared that the engine was a liter larger than it really was. I needed another official letter. Looking back it was apparent that the mistake was probably a deliberate invention by the clerk: Kevin Schulmeister.

The registration process was allowed to proceed. The registration office, 45 kilometers away, is only open three mornings a week and upon arrival 15 minutes after it opened, I was 70th in line. The office stopped dealing with people at number 46 to take lunch. New registrations were not taken in the afternoon.

The next day, I arrived 90 minutes before the office opened and was fifth in line so although I'd lost a little sleep I did complete the registration … this time with the help of a friendly government employee (surprise, surprise!). She accepted an owner's tax receipt as proof of ownership whereas she might have forced me to make a third visit with a copy of the car title, despite the title having been sent to her ministry in order to release the Ministry letter, which I had given her.

John Graham

Registration produced one rear license plate, however, the compulsory front number plate is the owner's own responsibility, of course, at additional cost. Paying thousands of euros in registration fees apparently doesn't cover the cost of two plates. A trip across the road got the mandatory front license plate for another €25. Neither fitted my car, which was made to accept US sized license plates. Ingenuity was needed to avoid drilling holes in the car.

Then a visit to the insurance agent provided coverage within a few minutes. The car was now legal and could be driven.

I decided to worry about the cost of registration and of insurance when the bills arrived, as I happily thought on my first legal drive. However, the registration certificate contained the same error ... claiming that the car had a 4-liter engine instead of a 3-liter. That little error made an immense difference to registration taxes and insurance fees so something was still needed. The Federal Ombudsman was recruited once more.

However, Socialist countries catch you coming or going. Despite being just 2,996 cc, the car generates 187kw of power compared to what appears to be the usual for down-rated Belgian cars with the same capacity. They generate about 120kw, so the tax is charged on capacity or power depending on which provides the most money to the government.

Of course, Ministries can require your response within a few days under pain of a fine, but you cannot require that they do their job in any time at all.

However the story continues.

The applicant was presented with a tax bill, for first putting the car on the road, and another tax sum for using it. He noticed that the tax was still based on it being a 3,996 cc engine so he objected. The lady at the office, one of the two helpful civil servants met in this sad tale, made enquiries and admitted that the bill was excessive but she couldn't make adjustments unless the applicant first paid the whole thing. Reluctantly, I did. She then announced that he had paid 1108.33€ too much and that would be refunded.

She said that the applicant could expect a letter formally announcing the overcharge in January and he would be repaid two months later. This was in October but he waited patiently. At the end of January he wrote again and was told that the responsibility had passed from Federal to Flemish authorities and that they would be dealing with the matter.

The applicant e-mailed everything to them … no answer.

He sent them a registered letter with everything … no answer.

Now it was time for the Ombudsman again.

The Ombudsman replied very quickly saying it was now the task of the Flemish Ombudsman and he gave me contact details. However, a letter to the new Ombudsman revealed that he could do nothing for 45 days. I also received a letter from the Finance Ministry saying that they had 45 days to act. On hearing that an Ombudsman was involved they had at least replied to the enquiries that had been ignored for four months even if they simply announced that they would do nothing for another month and a half.

In 38 days, the Taxation office responded saying that they tried to settle such complaints within six months. In the end they admitted fault and promised to repay their excessive tax claim before November, twenty-seven months after the arrival of the car on the docks at Antwerp. However, it had not yet finished!

They owed 1108.94€ but at the end of October, a new taxation office civil servant sent an e-mail noting that 118.94€ would transferred to my bank account. (Notice the difference!) It was also announced that the e-mail address that they had used was no longer available. For comment, the official Taxation website was recommended. Thus to correct the new thousand-euro error might take a further 45 days to consider a new comment.

Finally, however, through another e-mail address that had not been cut off, the money was repaid 27 months after the car had landed on the docks.

Now however there is the matter of interest earned on that excess tax. An invoice was presented for immediate payment (within two working weeks) of 5% interest. It was unlikely that any payment would be received but after 27 months of frustration one has to have a modicum of revenge, even by just being on the demand side. Friends advised against the bother.

Seventeen different offices of nine different organizations, all of which have different levels of bureaucratic inefficiency, had been involved. Only one person had been truly helpful although another might have succeeded if the requirements themselves were not antiquated and meaningless.

Having had at first no reply to my demand for interest on the money that had been owed, another letter was sent – this time with a threat:

"The time provided for repayment of the interest debt (55,45€) of the Flemish Ministry for illegally withholding 1108,94€ in taxes for over a year has exceeded the procedural allowance of ten working days. There has been no response to the claim submitted through the Ministry website.

The Ministry is now in default and is liable for penalty payments as well as interest.

A response is required within the next five working days (as per procedure) by November 18th, 2011. **If no response or payment is received by that date the claim will be presented through the public Belgian press and to the Minister, naming the recipients of this e-mail as being individually delinquent in their Ministry duties."**

Lo and behold! I then received an immediate reply saying that I was "indeed entitled to interest according to articles 418 and 419 of procedure WIB 92 and the Ministry would shortly pay 77.04€ into my account." While I had asked for a nominal 5%, they paid 7% because, in fact, they legally had to. However, they are not apparently forced to tell you that you are entitled to interest on their overcharge.

Thus, it is worth quoting the authority of 'procedures,' even if they are only your own, and to attach the idea of a visit to the press, naming names.

The problem of running into competitive Ministries (Federal and Flemish) doing the same job but having to do things in Dutch rather than to offend the French by speaking in English (and vice versa presumably), is simply archaic and backward-looking nonsense. However, if one ignores the local language and simply speaks and writes in English, everything is intelligible except that the reply is in Dutch. This practice is merely extremely bad manners and hardly endears the enquirer to pursuing an enquiry. It is a principle of good behaviour that an enquiry in one language should be answered in that language perhaps at the same time mentioning that one might be comfortable in another language.

Perhaps these language problems are an interim painful condition before Europe adopts a real common language. Unfortunately, the enforcement of a local dialect hampers business.

Then, apart from the problem of language, having three ministries performing the same tax collection job is obviously hugely uneconomic. This is Belgium but similar inefficiencies exist in Canada and in different areas of the United States such as Colorado and southern California.

In summary, expecting to be able to drive a car away from the docks was simply out of touch with bureaucratic Belgium. Belgium importation consists of a multitude of offices, none of which seem to communicate with another, and archaic regulations as well as their application by mostly anonymous unresponsive civil servants, including one with malicious intent.

Indeed, the Belgians would have easily defeated the Nazi Blitzkrieg at the beginning of World War II if they had stationed their multiple customs offices, the *autokeuring* road safety office and the multiple offices of the Ministry of Transport at the border. The German tanks would have still been at the border today trying to obtain entry.

This story is a sad reflection on clerks … even those who think themselves in elevated positions of authority. At best they can be considered government or company clerks, for that is how they are paid. They are not public or civil servants by any stretch of the imagination.

John Graham

Managing payment

Bribes are an avowed evil according to governments and to many companies.

They are not allowed.

However, in most countries, bribery is a way of doing business and it is difficult to make the distinction between passing along an envelope full of currency on one hand in Qatar and wining and dining a customer along with a gift for the wife In Washington, DC, on the other. That customer may well have been brought in a company jet and accommodated in a suitable hotel at government or company expense as well.

The difference, of course, is from which accounts the spending comes. No government or company show 'bribes' as a business overhead and yet it is widespread.[47] To deny that is simple hypocrisy.

Civil servants do not make much in the way of salary. Instead they are offered an assured job from which they can never be fired (unless in 2011 they happen to be Greek or Spanish or Italian), and a pension at the end of a fixed service life. Thus, the acquisition of a little more unbudgeted cash is irresistible, especially if all it means is doing their job just a little more efficiently.

In Belgium and the Netherlands

A car importer was naïve to believe that he would penetrate Belgium's myriad regulations and forms

---

[47] The author almost added a waiver, "especially in ..." but has to admit simply that it is widespread throughout the world.

needed to drive a car legally on European roads without bribery. He finally met an organization in the Netherlands whose purpose was to pass along bribes in return for expeditious service. His trials and tribulations would have been minimized if he had known that at the beginning of his import.

In another Belgian case, planning permission for flat-roofed home required that every owner in the locality be asked whether he or she agreed or not. Permission required 75% approval. Many owners were absentee owners, or owners who lived abroad, but the planning official in charge was adamant that each had to be contacted for an opinion. This was even though the area contained other flat-roofed homes. Naturally, the survey took a great deal of labor in writing letters and in visiting and revisiting homes and in dealing with recalcitrant owners. Furthermore, after it was all accomplished it was clear that two residents, wealthy business people, had not had to go through the same exercise. Bribes had clearly been passed. In this case however the planning official got no bribe so he wreaked his eventual spite by demanding full compliance with a nonsense regulation and by, reluctantly, issuing planning permission on the last day available to him and demanding that the notice be posted at the site immediately -- on Christmas day.

That is an example of a very frustrated civil servant who did not receive a bribe.

In England

In a different type of case, two officials of local city government visited the manager of a nursery garden, which also included the sale of trellis and paving stones with a small area dedicated to making the concrete tiles. They announced that they had come to investigate a rumour that a concrete factory was to be built on that site. They threatened immediate closure of the business.

No, they were not allowed to reveal the source of the rumour. No, neither did they need credentials announcing their visit or their requirements. However, they told the manager, "You could be out of a job within days."

The manager, by now in tears, phoned her employer who was not one to take unannounced inspections lightly. He is a Brit. He immediately drove across country to the nursery.

After an angry encounter in which the owner thoroughly rebuked the two for driving his manager to tears, he told them to ••••• off. He also announced that he had heard that a factory was to be built on the city's nationally important football field pitch and they should investigate that. He pointed out that they could not reveal the source of the rumour.

Then he told his manager to leave for the day and he threw the keys at the two officials of local government, saying "Lock up after you. I am off to see my Member of Parliament."

They followed him to his car and pleaded with him not to go, to take his keys back and be rational. He left.

The following day, the two officials returned to the nursery garden offering profuse apologies to the manager and announcing that they would not be back and that they were satisfied by their "investigation." They emphasized that there was no need to contact their local government department.

Apparently, the threat of a visit to the local Member of Parliament who might ask the town council which clerks were making unannounced investigations to follow rumors, was sufficient to call off the dogs.

Two greased palms to the tune of a few hundred pounds each would probably have had the same result. They would have then moved on to 'officially' shake down another business.

Great Britain's manner of conducting business, usually above board, is no proof against bribery.

Worse, recently, it has been revealed that staff of the now defunct 'News of the World' had bribed the London Metropolitan Police into looking the other way while they hacked the cell phones of notables. Such bribes at the lowest level might extend to an envelope left on a desk, while at the higher levels 'funding' might have been provided for special projects. [48]

Bribery is no new phenomenon. The lowest ranks of government servants have always been amenable to a little extra to persuade them to do their job efficiently and expeditiously. Taking something extra for doing that didn't even seem wrong.

In the United States

The institution of Prohibition in 1919 in the United States provides a good example.

---

[48] The author's father was a senior member of the London Metropolitan Police Force who assisted Lord Trenchard in rooting out corruption in the thirties. Corruption almost always involved bribery either in kind for lower ranks or in cash for the higher.

Staff was needed to administer new governance following passage of the 18th Constitutional Amendment banning alcohol. The Volstead Act provided the terms of the governance. Amongst its other provisions it stated that the Federal agents hired to enforce the law would not be formal qualified civil servants. This was because the 'dry' faction in Congress did not want 'wets' to be hired and then, because of civil service protection, be virtually impossible to get rid of. Thus the new Federal alcohol agents would merely be servants of government.

However, even without civil service protection there was no lack of applicants for the initial 4,000-strong enforcement force. They all realized that for people to drink liquor in spite of regulations, graft and bribery would be the order of the day. The 4,000 were willing to hold their hands out.

Mable Willebrandt served as Assistant Attorney General in charge of Prohibition enforcement and when she viewed her agents, she said, "*I refuse to believe that out of our one hundred and twenty million population*[49] *... it is impossible to find four thousand men in the United States who can not be bought.*" That was after eight years of trying.[50]

Thus the leaders of a society create governance but agents and clerical members administer that governance. Prohibition was tailor-made for inefficiency and graft but experience shows that the

---

[49] 120 million was the population of the United States in 1927 – it was 307 million in 2009

[50] "Last Call - the rise and fall of Prohibition," Daniel Okrent, Scribner, New York, June 2010, pp. 138-141

same goes in most applications of government. It is all a matter of degree.

When one has to apply for something supplied by government, be it local planning permission or the necessary certification to proceed to the next step in any process, it is worth remembering that an individual government employee is involved, and a bribe might save a lot of frustration.

This advice is not to recommend bribery as a way of doing business; it is simply to say that bribery happens. That person who has moved ahead of you in the queue may know the same thing.

understanding

Several times in this text mention has been made of the necessity for civil servants to act with 'understanding'.

In September 2011, 101-year-old woman, Texana Hollis, was evicted from the southwest Detroit home (a poor and depressed neighborhood) where she had lived for nearly six decades. Her 65-year-old son had failed to pay the mortgage.

When she had moved in she was in her early forties with a 7-year-old son. This day, conditions were different.

Texana Hollis was evicted on a Monday and her belongings were placed outside the home. Her son, Warren Hollis, said he hadn't paid the bill for several years and had disregarded eviction notices.

"I kept it from her because I didn't want to worry her," Warren Hollis told the local television station. "I was just so sure it (eviction) wasn't going to happen."

Wayne County Chief Deputy Treasurer David Szymanski told The Associated Press that the Hollises took out an adjustable-rate mortgage in 2002. A default and foreclosure notice was filed in November 2010.

"They ended up owing $80,000 on the home," Szymanski said. "Warren indicates he did not make the payments. He got the notices, but threw them away."

County records show that property taxes were paid on the home through the summer of 2010. A winter tax bill of $55.95 was owed but not delinquent and a $778.44 summer tax bill was due later.

So what did Wayne County Chief Deputy Treasurer David Szymanski do?

He presumably knew someone was living in the house since taxes had been paid until very recently.

He presumably knew that the occupants had lived there for nearly six decades.

Yet, with no more than mailed eviction notices he put the matter in the hands of a third-party eviction firm who physically put out the 101-year-old woman in her wheel chair with her belongings on the sidewalk outside the home. She didn't even have her medication.

It is no wonder that she was taken to a hospital for evaluation after she became disoriented.

Understanding requires that the civil servant do more than issue an eviction notice and wash his hands of the consequences.

Wayne County Chief Deputy Treasurer David Szymanski might first have found out whether his bills and eviction notices were being received by all parties to the mortgage and asked why they had been ignored. Since eviction is a last resort, he might have visited the property. He might have spoken to Texana Hollis and her son and assured himself that his notices were understood. He might have acted with a more humanity in the actual eviction by trying to understand what conditions the 101-year-old disabled woman could manage.

David Szymanski is one of the worst examples of a civil servant who, as a first step, should lose his position immediately and then be prosecuted for a number of offences. He acted with no understanding.

Speaking of understanding, do TSA minions really think people don't mind being fingered in public – especially by an oaf in a toy uniform?

Understanding is a reciprocal emotion so should the public try to understand the frustrations of being in a non-creative dead-end job all day and every day and of putting up with bloody-minded members of the public? Should they then tolerate the behaviour of civil servants, together with their lack of response and their mindless application of fatuous regulations?

My personal feeling is "No," and in most cases, "absolutely, bloody well, NO!"

As a practicing scientist in the past I was charged with performing accurate calculations, not those containing errors from lazy work. I remember once being appalled at finding an error. Similarly a civil servant dealing with the public has a responsibility to perform that job with the complete responsiveness and that means acknowledging the needs of the applicant.

Some applicants don't take it lying down.

Although physical attacks on civil and company servants are rare they are not unknown.

In one case, a young lady with a desperate need to make the next flight was being fobbed off by the usual explanations of delays and "I don't know, please sit down and wait," responses[51]. She leant across the

---

[51] United Airlines, Heathrow Airport, 1996

counter and took the airline employee by the collar of her uniform, and pulling her forward, looking into her eyes, said, "I need to be on that plane. Do you understand?"

Apparently this clear communication worked. Miraculously, a seat was found for her on that plane.

Novelists can take their anger further.

Hans Fallada's character in *"Little Man, What now?"* shows him as angry but compliant. It was in a period in which public anger would not be tolerated.

However, Peter Hoeg in *"The Quiet Girl"* ridicules his immigration interviewer by speaking to her in front of her staff about their past intimate but imaginary affair and then recoiling from her apparent advance and throwing himself on the floor giving the impression that she has attacked him. His claim that they had known each other sexually gained credibility. She was quickly relieved of her part in his review.

More violently, Peter Carey, in *"The Tax Inspector,"* murders the civil servant at the end of the story. On the occasion of a tax audit, two decades ago, having just read Peter Carey's book, I told the tax inspector about it and about its conclusion laughingly. On my next visit to her office I gave her my copy of Carey's book. Her acceptance of the book probably violated one of her codes of conduct and I had the satisfaction of expressing an implicit opinion about tax inspectors. The audit was successfully concluded, fairly soon afterwards, without penalty. Perhaps the book had a part in the solution.

However, most people take the incivility and inconsideration of civil servants very passively.

Murder may be in their hearts but not in their immediate future.

Sometimes people feel there is no way out.

In Texas Rachelle Grimmer, 38, pulled a gun on the welfare office supervisor, Roberto Reyes, and her two children out of her frustration at being denied food stamps.[52]

A SWAT team surrounded the building, and officers communicated with Grimmer throughout the ordeal. But at midnight -- shortly after Grimmer hung up on police -- three shots were fired, causing the police to storm the building.

Rachelle Grimmer was pronounced dead at the scene, while her daughter 12-year-old Ramie and her brother, Timothy, 10, suffered critical head wounds and were transported to University Hospital in San Antonio, according to the San Antonio Express.

Grimmer's outburst was reportedly triggered after years of getting rejected for state assistance in various states, the newspaper reported. The family had recently moved to Texas from Ohio.

Stephanie Goodman, a spokeswoman for the Texas Department of Health and Human Services, told ABCNews.com that Grimmer hadn't been rejected. She had just received a notice that her case was closed, since she did not provide all of the necessary documentation during the department's 30-day time frame. (I wonder what 'rejected' means?)

"She absolutely could have applied again," Goodman

---

[52] Alyssa Newcomb reporting for Good Morning America, December 8, 2011

said.

Neighbors said the Grimmers lived in a trailer about 6½ feet wide and 16 feet long.

"The children went barefoot to accompany her. They went four times, and four times she was denied. She was desperate, because she had nothing to feed her children," neighbor Oscar Luis Cuellar told the Laredo Sun.

Goodman said employees at the Laredo Office were struggling to cope in the aftermath of the shooting. "They're very badly shaken. They go into this business because they want to help people," she said. **"Even though it was processed according to our procedures, it does not comfort them at all."**

The employees at the Laredo Office apparently didn't understand that a mother and barefoot children who had been denied assistance four times already needed real help, well beyond 'procedures' or the 'comfort' they provide.

The Texas Department of Health and Human Services should be cleaned out immediately.

These examples should have clearly defined what makes a bad civil servant or in Goodman's case, a bad communicator. However, it's worthwhile considering what makes a bad civil servant a little more thoroughly.

What makes a bad civil servant?

Usually, what a civil servant, company representative or government employee is asked for is 'information.'

What a supplicant would like is accurate and useful information for the issue with which he or she is concerned. What he or she generally gets is partially relevant information accompanied by a direction to seek more information elsewhere. This advice is bounded by times and restrictions that take no account of the supplicant's particular case. He or she hardly ever gets information that recognizes his or her particular needs.

Moreover, don't hold the clerk responsible!

The following is a specific disclaimer,[53] which appears to be the manner in which most civil servants, government and company employees approach the idea of providing information to a member of the public.

"Limitation of Liability"

"Without waiving any other defenses or immunities provided by law, the Clerk shall not be liable for any demand or claim, regardless of form of action, arising

---

[53] Disclaimer Agreement, Howard C. Foreman, Clerk of the Courts, Broward County 17th Judicial Circuit of Florida. <ttp://www.clerk-17th-flcourts.org/ClerkWebsite/BCCOC2/Disclaimer.aspx>

out of or incident to the posting of information or data on this website, the accessing or use of any information or data on this web site, and/or the acts or omissions of any person or entity accessing or use of any information from this web site. This includes, but is not limited to, claims arising out of or incident to incorrect or incomplete data or information accessed pursuant to this Disclaimer Agreement. All users are advised to independently verify any information or data obtained pursuant to this Disclaimer Agreement with the official court record information reposing in the court files. User agrees that the services are provided "as is"; neither clerk, the custodians and/or their third-party providers make any representation nor warranty with respect to accuracy, completeness, or currentness (Sic); and they specifically disclaim any other warranty, express, implied or statutory, including any warranty of merchantability or fitness for a particular purpose. Neither the clerk, its officers, employees and agents, nor the custodians of records being accessed expressly or impliedly warrant that the information or data accessed by user is accurate or correct. There are no expressed or implied warranties in connection with this service. They shall not be liable on account of any such errors, omissions, delays, or losses. User agrees that in no event will clerk, the custodians and/or their third-party providers be liable for the results of user's use of the services, inability or failure to conduct its business, or for indirect, special or consequential damages. The foregoing limitation of liability and exclusion of certain damages shall apply regardless of the success or effectiveness of other remedies."

"User hereby relieves and releases Clerk, it officers, employees, agents, and the Custodians from liability from any and all damages resulting from interrupted service of any kind. Nothing in this agreement shall be construed as

waiving the sovereign immunity of Clerk, its officers, employees and agents, and the Custodians."

Now, what was it that you wanted?

On the other hand, some communicators are more than willing to tell all they know, but they too want to waive their responsibility. A common waiver is contained in the news article:

One of the most common reports of civil service communication read as something like this: "A law enforcement official, who spoke to the Associated Press on condition of anonymity because he was not authorized to discuss the case, said initial reports indicated that …"

It means, "I am not allowed to say anything and since I am a responsible official don't mention my name, but here is what I know."

Would you trust that person for any communication?

Let's get back to the question: first and foremost a civil servant is bad when he or she fails to take responsibility for the job they are paid to do, which is principally to provide information but sometimes can require action.

A very simple example at the lowest possible level of civil service will suffice.

A written request, for rented garbage disposal-can, that was not needed, to be picked up to avoid a monthly rental charge, was sent through the town hall. It met with absolutely no response after two weeks. An investigation found that although the clerk knew a disposal-can existed at the address and what size it was, she had seen that it was in the name of the wife not the husband who had signed the request for it to be taken away, so she did nothing. She simply laid the request aside. She made no enquiry, and placed no simple phone call, even though she had the number. She never, for one moment, thought of the person who made the request or why the request was made.

A similar example involved a file documenting a car for import through Customs. At the ministry the file was mistakenly completed with the wrong engine capacity. E-mails and a registered letter to inform them of the error simply went unanswered. It took the Federal Ombudsman to get a reply and then to have a revised file issued. However, even though the false file had originally been sent on to the taxation department by the ministry, no revised file was sent, so the taxation department were not informed of the change. This caused more than a year's delay in settling the tax for the vehicle. The clerk involved never considered the consequences of his lack of action on the person involved – or perhaps he did. A malicious action is not unknown.

A further example: a beautiful example of the inadequacy of government and the indolence of 'civil' servants. This is an example of lack of initiative and lack of pride in their position.

There is a new modern post office in a town in the north of Belgium. It is surrounded by a nominal 'garden' of clipped bushes, roses and ground cover. Not exactly my garden but it is a government office and it could be neat and tidy. However, today the clipped bushes were entirely hidden by an overgrowth of Convolvulus, while three-foot-high thistles and other large weeds had invaded the ground cover. I knew the ground cover was there but it couldn't be seen. Climbing weeds covered the roses. The place was an absolute mess, although half an hour would have cleared most of it.

There were two clerks in the office chatting to each other. I was their only mid-morning customer for stamps and I mentioned that they could do with a gardener. The response was, "Oh! That's a Brussels' problem. They select post offices for fronts to be cleared about every three months."

Apart from the stupidity of having local yard clearance administered from the nation's capital 90 kilometers away these two under-worked clerks were willing to sit and chat when they could quite easily have spent 15 minutes each uprooting a few large weeds. They clearly had no pride in their location. "That's a Brussels' problem," was sufficient excuse for them. They even looked a little aggrieved that no one was caring for them.

But these are small examples of civil servants who do the minimum that they need and only then when forced. There are other issues.

A civil servant administers a government policy, either by defining a procedure or simply issuing a form and filing it after completion. If asked, bad civil servants will say that it's not their responsibility to do more. They would not consider putting themselves in the shoes of the person they are dealing with; or having an opinion as to the fairness involved; or doing more than filling the hours before quitting time.

Bad civil servants also do not listen.

What better example of this trait than to go to a hearing clinic.

This explains how to make an appointment at a Hospital's audio clinic in the south of England. The sufferer explains:

"I thought I should have my hearing tested … based on the number of times I have to ask my wife to repeat something she said. (Mind you, quite often she holds a conversation with me from another room.) My doctor said he would arrange for a hearing test for me."

"Two weeks later I had a letter from the hospital clinic giving me an appointment on September 14th."

"This was not convenient as I would be on a canal-boat holiday at that time so I telephoned, explained why the 14th was no good for me, and after a fairly lengthy wait on the telephone (a call I was paying for) was told they could arrange a hearing test for me on October 4th. "This," I said, "is fine", and foolishly thought that was the end of the matter."

"A week later, I had another letter from the clinic this time apologising for the fact that it was now not possible to fit me in on October 4th, but proudly announcing that they had booked me in for September 14th again."

"More 'phone calls, more frustration as I once again explained that I was on vacation on September 14th. I was told they would try and sort out another date. After a ten-day wait a letter dropped on my doormat again offering me October 4th. Suddenly, this date had become available for me again."

"I now await a further letter cancelling that and offering me September 14th again. Nothing would surprise me."

The sufferer asked the Hearing clinic representative to do two things… add him to one date and cancel him from another. That sounds beyond the capabilities of some of these institutional representatives. The appointment sounds ripe for disaster especially since it has been arranged by phone and mail. He probably should check that they haven't put him down for root-canal work in the hospital's Dental clinic by mistake.

It pays to be very careful when dealing with anonymous representatives.

An Invasive Organization

Inspectors of the Transport Security Administration in the United States and their supervisors are the very epitome of what makes a bad civil servant. Not only do they demean the member of the public before them but they also take pride in such behaviour since they are taught that they are thereby saving a nation.

There appears to be no Code of Conduct for TSA employees in their interaction with members of the public, although there is a means of submitting complaints, which are apparently expected. (There is a TSA Ombudsman but he has no responsibility for helping a member of the public.[54])

In the TSA Code of Responsibilities and Conduct for an employee there are three references to the public: the first is almost an afterthought while the second and third both express the Administration's concerns for the Administration rather than the public.

---

[54] Transport Security Administration (TSA), http://www.tsa.gov/

- Exercise courtesy and tact in dealing with fellow workers, supervisors, contract personnel (whether on or off-duty) and the public. Support and assist in creating a productive and hospitable model work environment. [55]
- Employees in direct contact with the public bear a heavy responsibility, as their conduct and appearance have a significant impact on the public's attitude toward the Federal government and TSA.[56]
- While on or off-duty, employees are expected to conduct themselves in a manner that does not adversely reflect on TSA, or negatively impact its ability to discharge its mission, cause embarrassment to the agency, or cause the public and/or TSA to question the employee's reliability, judgment or trustworthiness.

Guidance is given for employees needing to report their own criminal infractions but nowhere is there guidance on how an employee should conduct their dealings with the public. It is no wonder that a TSA employee is typically a very bad civil servant.

Other civil servants simply do not believe their duty extends to helping someone so much as performing the tiny task in which they are entrusted.

---

[55] TSA Management Directive No. 1100.73-5 Employee Responsibilities and Conduct. Item 5(3)

[56] TSA Management Directive No. 1100.73-5 Employee Responsibilities and Conduct. Item 6B

One such person had the responsibility of invoicing for a tax payment. Apparently it was not her job to confirm that the tax she was charging was correct even though the taxpayer wanted to know because in the prior year a serious mistake had been made. She advised the enquirer to write to another office (in the same building) for information if he wanted to know more. Fortunately, he didn't take the brush off. He wrote a stern letter back, copying the Ombudsman and requesting that she should supply the information he had requested within three days "as per procedure." Of course, the procedure he mentioned was his own rather than her department's but the letter implied that if the information were not forthcoming further action would be taken.

He was sent the information that he wanted within a couple of hours. It certainly hadn't taken the woman long to produce a link to a site explaining the charges.

Remember that Adolf Eichmann was a civil servant given the responsibility of implementing the government policies of eliminating undesirables: Jews, gypsies, disabled persons, homosexuals and criminals.

He was thorough and he did his job well.

He was dispassionate. He never once put himself in the position of the young woman stripped of her clothes and belongings standing nude in the snow at Auschwitz with her head shorn. He never once put himself in the shoes of a Jewish child taken from its mother and transported to a gas chamber. He never once had an ounce of shame, even at his trial, although he certainly knew that he was guilty by virtue of his years in hiding.

Of course, all civil servants are not Eichmanns but the worst show all the same uninvolved and unsympathetic characteristics. Put into the same position at Auschwitz they might equally excel.

The dangers of uncorrected civil service behavior

Tristan Jones had vast experience with minor officials, mostly from customs and immigration, when he sailed a yacht with occasional cross-land adventures from 1,250 feet below sea-level on the Dead Sea to over 12,500 feet on Lake Titicata in Peru before dragging the yacht back to the Atlantic Ocean through the wetlands of the Matto Grosso.[57] He crossed many international borders and knew well how minor officials get into power and bring their "uninvolved and unsympathetic characteristics" with them.

From Lake Titicata, where Peruvian officials demanded half the value of his yacht, the Sea Dart, for allowing its transit across the country, he launched by river towards the Atlantic ocean, thus escaping their clutches.

In traversing Brazil's Matto Grosso, often times dragging the yacht by hand through small streams and swamps, he had arrived in San Lazaro, Paraguay. There 304,000 men had died for the town in the Paraguayan War of the Triple Alliance. There was yet another Customs office to visit. There was yet another customs official to confront.

He didn't approach the prospect very positively!

---

[57] "*The Incredible Voyage – a Personal Odyssey*," Tristan Jones, 1976, page 344.

"And I thought what assholes get into power. How these bastards work their way up by stages, like woodworms eating their way through furniture, like teredo worms gnawing through a rotten keel, from behind their anonymous desks, where they gradually build up their secret little empires and weave their sticky webs of intrigue until suddenly, almost unnoticed until the very last minute, they are in control. Then there we are, under the heel of fucking maniacs like Stalin (originally the People's Commissar for Nationalities' Affairs), Mussolini (an office worker for the local socialist party), Hitler (son of a Custom's official), Franco (in charge of supplies), Peron, Trujillo, Stroessner, Kadaffi, and Idi Amin. The list goes on and on. And the only reason these buggers ever get to the top is because few people will stand on the rooftop and shout, "Hey, look what's happening! Look at this little asshole crawling his way up!"[58]

Often these people use the army for their ascent, but others take their inhumanity into politics as they ascend the civil-service ladder or its equivalent in other countries.

These are the worst of the worst. Generally, most of us simply meet civil servants who are rude and intolerant and treat as an imposition on their day.

A quick search of the Internet provided 8.3 million hits in a search for 'rude civil servants'. While such a volume of hits is highly repetitive, nevertheless a rude civil servant is not a rare occurrence. Furthermore, the

---

[58] *"The Fantastic Voyage – a Personal Odyssey,"* Tristan Jones, Sheridan Books, 1996

complaints extend throughout Asia, from Japan[59] to Borneo, and right across Europe and the United States.

Nowhere is remote from rude civil servants.

China

From China[60] comes a typical example of the reluctance of civil servants to encroach upon 'their time'.

In June 2011, an applicant to an office from Guangzhou wrote criticizing the rude attitude of a civil servant in the office of Legislative Affairs in Guangzhou, and also uploaded a sound recording onto the Internet that showed the conflict between the applicant and the civil servant, Peng Hui, in the office.

The applicant said, at 11:30 a.m. of June 17, he went, with another house owner (female) on behalf of all the house owners in their residential block, to the office of

---

[59] "Okinawa Prefecture officials are warning rude civil servants at public offices to change their ways. The prefecture has created a new office, the so-called "Fresh Service Office", to receive complaints on the matter from the public and then giving guidance to civil servants where necessary.

According to Ryusei Tomoyose, the Fresh Service Office Head, the most frequent complaints from the public are dirty toilets, followed by a lack of reserved parking for the handicapped, not enough maps informing the public of office locations and slow service."

[60] China Buzz – news of happenings in China, <http://www.chinabuzz.net>

legislative affairs to apply for an administrative review, but was rejected by the staff in the office. The staff told them to come again in the afternoon, because the office wouldn't handle any case after 11:30 a.m.

The applicant complained, "State Law regulates that the working-time of civil servants in the morning is until 12:00 a.m. How can you refuse our case when we still have half of an hour?"

According to the recording, a man with local accent, after being questioned, lost his temper and shouted, "I have explained to you, 11:30-12:00 is our working time, but I do not accept any case now. This is our internal work time. You can't intervene."

The applicant also said, when they criticized the man for not behaving as required by the code of conduct for civil servants, and that he should not rage and roar at citizens, the man even responded, "That is my right. So what? What can you do about it?"

Then another civil servant threatened that he would call the security guards and police.

Furthermore, from 11:30 to 12:00, no senior civil servants in the office came to investigate the matter.

The experience sounds remarkably similar to other experiences in Denver, Colorado.

What makes a good civil servant?

To provide a little background to this question, note that a search for examples of 'rude civil servants' on the Internet scored 8.3 million hits, while a search for examples of 'courteous civil servants' scored zero. A good civil servant or good public servant is a very rare bird indeed.

Clearly a good civil servant is opposite to a bad civil servant. It simply takes "walking a mile in the applicant's moccasins." That might involve walking around the intervening desk and other barriers; it might involve translating some of the department's special terms and acronyms; it might involve leaving one's ego and pride at home; it might be extremely difficult for many people.

The International Civil Service Commission, in 2002, took it upon itself to produce Standards of Conduct for the International Civil Service[61] that could have been considered as examples of standards that could be used across the world. There are fifty standards but only four (4) treat the relationship of civil servants with the public.

These four standards deal first with promoting the work of the civil servant's division of the government, second their right to be defended against criticism and third that they should not criticize their own organization. The fourth finally notes that civil servants 'should be tolerant of other races, customs

---

[61] **Standards of Conduct for the International Civil Service,** International Civil Service Commission, Chairman: Mohsen Bel Hadj Amor, January 2002

and traditions.' There is no intimation that a civil servant should deal with a member of the public with understanding and respect befitting that individual. 'Tolerance' is a very faint measure of respect.

There are, however, eleven (11) standards defining that the civil servant should not gain through bribery or dishonest practices or employment concurrent with their service as a public servant. These issues seem to be a relatively large problem in the commission's collective mind.

Fortunately, there are also written standards for civil servants in many countries.[62]

Jolanta Palidauskaite,[63] of Kaunas University of Technology, Lithuania, refers to standards in Eastern Europe:

"Codes of conduct for public servants in Eastern and Central European countries are rather new phenomena. Newly established democracies are (just now) building their administrative systems, creating legal frameworks and administrative traditions."

"The indifference with regard to the public, arrogant behaviour and servile attitudes, and slowness that were common during the communist era are still often met in the activity of public servants in the region. A

---

[62] Australia, Brazil, Canada, Greece, Italy, Korea, New Zealand, Poland, Spain, United Kingdom, United States.

[63] **"Codes of Conduct for Public Servants in Eastern and Central European Countries: A Comparative Perspective,"** Jolanta Palidauskaite, OECD, oecd.org/dataoecd/17/32/35521438.pdf

bureaucratic attitude and an individualist culture are the main threats to the public interest. Frequent changes of ministers have led to unstable working conditions and the result is a lack of motivation and indifference by public servants to the results of their work. Despite these features, some progress in public service ethos is evident. Changes have mainly occurred as a result of external pressures, in particular the EU enlargement process, and increasing demands from the public."

"Government in transitional societies is starting to understand the importance of officials' ethical conduct on a day-by-day basis. The proof of it are newly adopted public service acts, laws on conflict of interest, anticorruption strategies, and codes of conduct or ethical codes."

"Ethical aspects of public servants behaviour in Estonia, Latvia, Poland, Czech Republic, Bulgaria, Macedonia are regulated formally through the existing laws and informally with the help of codes of conduct."

"Ethical aspects in Hungary, Croatia, and Slovenian Republic are regulated through the existing laws Lithuania, Serbia, Slovakia, Albania and Romania are still in the process of developing their professional codes of conduct."

"Estonia was the first of the Baltic countries and in the region to adopt Public Service Code of Ethics in 1999."

Palidauskaite's reference to "The indifference with regard to the public, arrogant behaviour and servile attitudes, and slowness that were common during the communist era are still often met in the activity of public servants in the region" should be amended to include the same behavior throughout the world.

Interestingly, neither Belgium nor The Netherlands has Codes of Conduct for their civil servants. It shows.

How effective are these codes of conduct?

The following are an excerpt from standards written for Irish Civil Servants. Unfortunately, the "Dealings with the Public" are the briefest of the 21 Standards set. The others deal with the acceptance of gifts and hospitality and involvement in politics and the law and conflicts of interest and payment by others. Bribery is a real issue with civil servants

Here are the few words for dealing with the public. Compliance makes the person a good civil servant.

"8. Dealings with the public. [64]

8.1 Civil servants should:

- Ensure that members of the public have their affairs dealt with sympathetically, efficiently and promptly;

- Always give their names to any member of the public with whom they are dealing, except where given a special exemption, for example on security grounds, and

- Ensure that members of the public are dealt with in a respectful manner.

---

[64] Standards in Public Office Commission, Ireland,
http://www.sipo.gov.ie/en/CodesofConduct/CivilServants/

8.2 Civil servants should:

- Ensure that their standard of dress is appropriate to their work environment;

- Show due consideration and respect for the public, their colleagues and the office they hold."

Paragraph 8.1 is the most proactive standard of conduct that we have found anywhere. 'Sympathy' and 'respect' are mentioned. 'Understanding' is not. However, a good civil or public servant puts himself or herself in the other person's shoes. It's rare but it does happen.

On another level in the Irish standards, efficiency and promptness are mentioned, but these are simply rules of business and should always apply whether or not the person is dealing with the public.

The idea of a civil servant giving his name is a good one because it establishes some sort of personal contact. However, experience shows that this is rarely done unless the supplicant demands the person's name with the idea of complaining. That's why personal names are not generally revealed.

Occasionally, one meets a representative of government who leaves a pleasurable impression. The operative word is 'occasionally' because such experiences are not the norm.

There are some common characteristics of such a person.

First, this good civil servant deals with the public and meets the man or woman affected by their actions, up close and in person. The supplicant becomes a real person, dressed in real clothes with bright eyes, a smile or a worried look with maybe an untidy haircut, rather than being simply an anonymous 'John Doe' supplicant.

On the other hand, civil servants charged with doing something to a piece of paper before putting it into the out-tray never see the person involved and have no idea of the consequences of their actions, although they have been told to act strictly according to the regulations. Having to deal with real people in person seems to make civil servants more human.

Secondly, the person is usually young and new to the job. They are keen to do a good job and haven't yet been borne down by the sheer weight, unintelligibility and often, sheer inhumanity or inanity of regulations. Often, they will try to help even if only by pointing to a less ponderous way through their own regulations.

One group of people who are constantly in contact with the public either as technical 'experts' or to explain business products who are uniformly excellent at listening to people and finding the right and helpful answers are the employees of Apple stores. They are all young and being divided into two classes: the business and technical sides, they easily pass off questions to another more qualified person. I have never had experience of an arrogant Apple representative, nor a rude one, nor an impatient one. It is amazing but one always emerges from an Apple store feeling pleased that you received the straight story whether you bought something or not. There is a hierarchy amongst the Apple employees but it rarely shows. Each appears to be fully competent within their area of expertise. This applies whether the encounter is in a store, through the Internet or by phone. Apple clearly has mastered another product that they could happily market, especially to the government, the polite, patient and knowledgeable public contact.

Unfortunately, in government circles those young people who are new and keen on doing a good job will almost certainly become older and keen more on their ability to draw a pension after 30 years. Their colleagues will point to the fact that there is no reward for initiative or for thinking further than their particular regulation. A fresh young helpful civil servant doesn't last long.

It is easy to recognize good civil servants. First and foremost, they communicate … by answering questions helpfully in person, by phone, through electronic mail, and they try to respond to the question that they have been asked as if they had asked it themselves. It sounds so easy.

However, these are those who do not treat a member of the public as anything more than an intolerable disturbance to their day.

Of course, there is an element of Catch 22 in the question of what makes a good civil servant since a really intelligent and serving person would probably not be in the job in the first place. Instead, they might work in a school or a hospital or a private service agency where the welfare of their client is their number-one priority.

On another occasion, in Colorado, a very sick child was taken to a hospital emergency room on a Sunday. Both the doctor and the clerk at the desk treated her as the only person that mattered. Even without the X-ray procedure and the subsequent medication their attitude and approach was curative and she felt better immediately. If she had been treated as a number in the waiting room as so often happens that wouldn't have been the result.

In Belgium, the applicant was sitting in his car in a very long line of cars awaiting entry to the safety testing station (*autokeuring*). He had been told that he had to get his car tested for its safety before he could apply for registration and since his car was a virtually new BMW that didn't seem a problem. What he had not been told was that he needed a number of pieces of paper before he could have his car safety tested (such as those confirming his residence, the actual capacity of the car's engine, and insurance and more). Thus, he didn't know that the hour or more he seemed to be condemned to wait for his turn would be wasted.

Fortunately, this station had a conscientious and responsible civil servant at its head.

As soon as safety testing had started, the '*Chef*' walked down the line of waiting cars and poked his head in at each window. His message was simple, "If you don't have the right paperwork, I have to turn you away." Moreover, he was very willing to tell each driver what pieces of paper he needed.

This applicant had almost none so the *Chef* said, "Come back when you've got this and this and this. It'll save you time. Look you can turn around here to get out easily."

He saved the applicant an hour or more, who left to go home feeling a little more in charge. The *Chef* probably saved himself or his employees a little hassle too, by being a responsible person going out of his way to solve a problem that he knew might arise.

He is an example of a good civil servant. Others might have sat in the *chef*'s office and left it to the first safety tester to refuse the applicant after a long wait.

Organizations often test their employees for performance but hardly ever for their relationship to their public.

One, in Nigeria[65] came to the conclusion that there was little to choose between the performance of males and females. However, the performance tests rated dressing appropriately, arriving at work on time, general ability, and effectiveness of communications, human relations, character traits, work habits and leadership attainment. They were measured categories and the conclusion, since they never measured how these civil servants treated supplicants, was simply that women were as bad as men at their job. There was no suggestion that users of their services were questioned and furthermore some of the performance parameters were based on video games. Unreal!

Indeed, it seems that Government departments and businesses don't know how badly the interaction of their employees with the public reflects on what they might do. For example the person who imported his car knows that Belgian Customs, Belgian Automobile Authorities and Belgian and Flemish Financial Ministries operate to standards no better than those of Soviet organizations back in the 70s. This is because their civil servants have no respect or understanding for the people whom they are supposed to serve.

---

[65] GENDER DIFFERENCES, BEHAVIOUR PATTERNS AND JOB PERFORMANCE OF FEDERAL CIVIL SERVANTS IN NIGERIA, L. A. Yahaya, Department of Educational Guidance and Counselling, University of Ilorin, Ilorin.

John Graham

With the shoe on the other foot

So far this book this book has dealt with cases in which the member of the public is the applicant or supplicant seeking information. Suppose now the civil servant wants information from a citizen.

In the United States

A citizen has protection under the Fourth Amendment to the U.S. Constitution against unreasonable questioning and search.[66] In particular, it protects personal privacy, and every citizen's right to be free from 'unreasonable government intrusion into their persons, homes, businesses, and property'. It would, for example, provide individual protection against police questioning one on the street without probable cause.

Notice that the Amendment protects against government intrusion and the parts of the government who might intrude are the Tax authorities (the Internal Revenue Service) or the Police in all its various forms from the Federal Bureau of Investigation to the Central Intelligence Agency to the State and Local Police. Government workers from Social Security or Welfare Departments are not likely to be involved unless a child is involved.

In theory, the police cannot question an individual unless there is suspicion that that individual has been involved in a crime and they cannot enter a house with a warrant signed by a judge.

---

[66] http://en.wikipedia.org/wiki/Fourth_Amendment_to_the_United _States_Constitution

In theory too the government agent must provide documentation concerning what information he or she is looking for.

The Fifth Amendment of the U.S. Constitution goes a little further by protecting the citizen against self-indictment. He cannot be witness against himself, in other words a citizen can simply refuse to answer a question if he thinks it is incriminating.

Since these protections arose[67] from English Common Law dating back to the Magna Carta of 1215, the same rights apply in the United Kingdom and in all the Commonwealth Countries as well as in many other nations who have copied English Common Law.

That's the theory, but in practice both tax authorities and police authorities have teeth. It is unwise to be recalcitrant unless one has something serious to hide and/or one has an excellent lawyer. The authorities might have a much more serious bite when they return with the right pieces of paperwork.

Courtesy is always good practice in dealing with the police at any level, even if the officer, a public servant, is not courteous.

In Britain

One has to be sensible. On one occasion when a person was carrying a large parcel through London streets at 1:30 a.m., he was stopped and asked by a policeman what was in the parcel. That seemed reasonable. It could have been a stolen article. It was not … it was a sleeping bag and the carrier had missed

---

[67] Fifth Amendment to the US Constitution, http://en.wikipedia.org/wiki/Fifth_Amendment_to_the_United_States_Constitution

his last Underground train. Furthermore, objecting to the question would probably have resulted in having to visit a police station or risk being charged with 'resisting arrest.' Courtesies were exchanged and the carrier went on his way without much delay.

If one would have preferred to be indignant or even aggressive it is better practice to exercise these emotions later.

In extreme occasions, questioning the training of the civil servant is a very reliable option since training provided to government and company front persons is very often deficient or absent. This is of course the whole problem being exposed by this text.

Everywhere

There is one other piece of important advice that should be emphasized.

Never, ever, tell a civil servant or an officer of any form of government, however pleasant they may seem, any more than they absolutely need to know. Never mention funds, income, bank accounts, credit cards, health, possessions or personal information. While small items could slip out in a private conversation with friends, civil servants should not be given any confidence since regulations might often hang you.

For example, even saying that one is a writer leads to an interest in what do you sell, in how you price, in where your books are published, in how much do you get paid, in where do those funds go, in how taxes are paid, in whether you charge a purchaser the VAT cost, in whether you have a VAT number, and so on and on. These are questions that no one should be asking unless you give a careless input. Be well aware to whom you are speaking. Once even a small amount of this information is recorded in some innocuous government file it can lead to other matters.

It is an established principle in the U.S. that if tax authorities ask to check on one item, no other item should be mentioned because that opens the door to what can be further enquired about. If you meet with a tax inspector any papers you take along should be strictly limited to the subject asked. Never take your full files. The same principle should be applied in your meetings with all civil servants.

For example, in applying for a renewal of your passport, never mention any other citizenship you may hold.

General observation

When one does meet a competent and patient civil or company servant, the good attitude reflects on the whole interaction. It is difficult to be angry at someone who is clearly doing their best to help you. It takes two to tango, but in these interactions one good civil servant who knows their job and tries to help can lead the dance.

The Fuzzy bit

Two people interact.

One has been trained to do the job, to provide information and to channel that information as responses to expected questions. In a sense this person starts with an FAQ[68] list in mind. These are not questions that are 'frequently asked' … they are a set of questions for which this person has an answer or at least a partial answer very often backed by a regulation. He or she would like every enquirer to fit into the pattern of asking one of these questions. In this way he or she will be successful, solving one enquiry quickly and dispassionately, before moving on to the next.

The other person has a question or a need in mind. It is singular and unique and, generally, it is a vague cloud of enquiry. It is very unlikely that it forms a neat item that slots into a FAQ list. He or she comes with a crumpled shopping list that has a very poor probability of fitting into the slot of the civil servant's receptor. Furthermore, this cloud of enquiry has associated concerns unique to the enquirer, such as how is this going to affect his mother-in-law or next Saturday's commitment to take his son to soccer.

Thus, this interaction is at best not made in heaven. It is more akin to fitting a peg into a slit or fitting a balloon into a keyhole. It is fraught with difficulty from the word "Go!"

Having heard the poorly framed enquiry, should the responder perhaps try to determine the outer edges of why the question has been asked, rather than try to fit

---

[68] FAQ -- Frequently Asked Questions

it into a narrow slit of a regulation? Should, on the other hand, the enquirer recognize the narrow focus of regulations and responses and try to compress his or her cloud?

The answer in both cases is "Yes." It would certainly help.

However, the title of this chapter is not chosen idly. It is a classic example from the science of Information Theory.[69] 'Fuzzy bits' are the ingredients of cryptology and the basis of new physics. The information from enquirer to responder can be interpreted only if they first agree on how it is to be done – that is, the enquirer sends the responder a code instruction beforehand. The pair has to be on the same page.

If they are not, the result is chaos.

Furthermore, each must recognize their part in this interaction: that one comes along with a cloud of queries and the other is equipped with package of index cards of answers. It is, looking at the meeting dispassionately, not made for success.

It would help enormously to understand one's part in this meeting, because of course the same frustrations and anger will appear if only one of the pair has this idea.

Notice that 'fuzzy bits' can only become interpretable information if the enquirer sends a codebook ahead of time. Thus, it is the enquirer's responsibility to explain the ramifications of his or her question and the responder should be patient enough to listen.

---

[69] "The Information", James Gleick, Pantheon Books, New York, 2011

So, why doesn't it work?

One reason is that the internal structure of a government or even a company organization often looks like this:

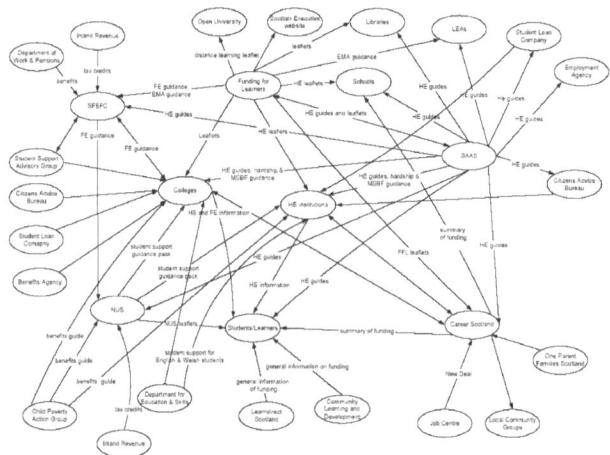

Even the representatives of the organization have little idea of how it works and so providing meaningful information for an outsider on related questions is almost impossible. This example of an organizational relationship relates to Scottish education.[70] Here the educational shepherds look more like the herd of sheep.

Often an organization is so complex, having grown like Topsy[71], that no employee quite knows what happens when a message is sent from a to b. In one

---

[70] Scottish Government, Information, Advice and Guidance Information flow, http://www.scotland.gov.uk/

[71] Unplanned growth, from Harriet Beecher Stowe's "Uncle Tom's Cabin" 1852

Belgian example, a specification that was in error was eventually corrected. However, although the original erroneous specification had been passed down the line for finance to take care of taxes, the revised specification never followed. It was simply filed.

An alternative organization is the following. It is very simple and it refers to Forestry data flow[72].

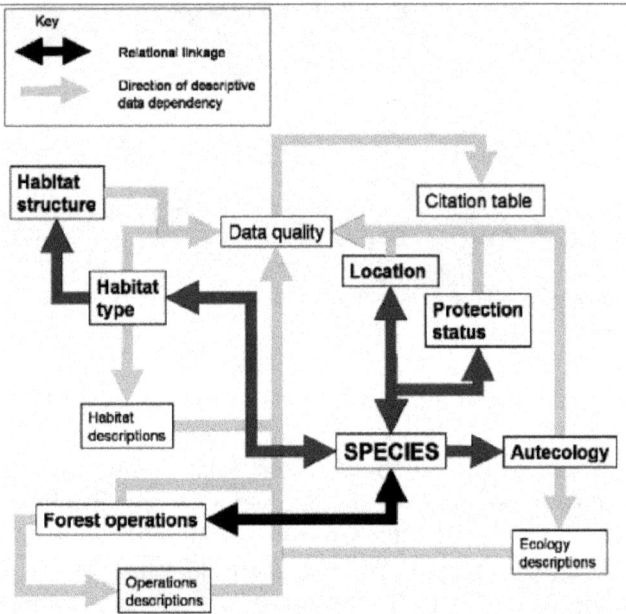

Notice that it neither allows input or nor does it provide any opportunity to question what data is being collected or why? It is based on the idea that the most efficient contact with the outside world is none.

_____

[72] Habitats and Rare Priority Protected Species Data Flow, http://www.forestry.gov.uk/fr/INFD-75LF88

These two examples are offered by way of humorous illustrations of serious issues. However, the second even contains some errors: apparently habitat affects data quality without even a description of the habitat, as do forest operations. This seems to have been unnoticed even by the speaker explaining the system.

Thus, remember when you approach a civil servant that initially you are almost certainly not on the same page. It may be as well to provide an introduction to your side of the issue before proceeding with the fuzzy bit.

The following is excellent advice in attempting to stay on the same page:

Steering your way through a dispute[73]

1. Before contacting a government agency to discuss a specific issue, make sure you have all the relevant documentation at hand.
2. Ask for a step-by-step list of the process you need to follow and keep to this list as best you can.
3. Ask for time frames to better gauge when you can expect to receive a reply.
4. To help you keep track of the progress of your issue and the people you have dealt with, keep a written record of your conversations, including the date, a summary of what was discussed and contact details.
5. Ask to speak to the same person each time you contact the agency.
6. Don't be hesitant in asking for further

---

[73] Small Business Development Association: Western Australia <http://www.smallbusiness.wa.gov.au/tips-for-dealing-with-government/#top>

information. For example, if you are experiencing delays, ask why.

7. Follow up regularly with the agency to find out how your query is being processed.

8. If you reach an agreement verbally, ask for confirmation in writing, by email or letter. If this is not possible, send an email or letter to confirm the agreement in writing and request an acknowledgement of receipt.

Unfortunately, while this sounds excellent advice many of these bullets prove to be impossible with the worst civil servants at the worst associations and government offices. In particular, one is unlikely to be able to accomplish much with items 2 and 3 because in all likelihood the person you are dealing with doesn't know the answers. Item 5 is almost never possible and the responses in the case of item 7 will be so vague as to be useless. Fallada's hero Pinneberg discovered that.

In summary

This book could be written off as a wordy case of sour grapes. In one sense it is … on behalf of us all. We have all suffered at the hands of uninvolved clerks and callous public servants at various levels in different organizations.

However, I hope that the book is a little more than sour grapes.

A 'Society' comprises people who want to live together for some geographical, historical, social, religious or ethical reason. For their wellbeing they need governance that defines their society and the rules whereby their society lives. Some, not many, governance employees, social servants and civil servants and company representatives, are needed to explain and to administer those rules.

Often a civil servant, or their equivalent in private business, will claim that if they do not administer rules strictly then the people they meet in their job will take advantage of them.

There are, naturally, those who want to take advantage of any system and who are quite likely to recognize a civil servant who wants to help as a way to gain an edge. Furthermore, one cannot expect civil servants to be responsible for the honesty of those who come to their counters. They are not the police, nor are they judge and jury of the approach that is being made to them. However, be that as it may, is it too much to expect that those government servants or civil servants act within their rules with responsibility, civility and understanding, even though the person opposite them may not be entirely honest? We all have the same decision to make in our own lives.

Apparently, in general, it is too much for civil servants!

Most countries see this issue as such an endemic problem that they have instituted codes of conduct for their civil servants. It is clear though that these have little effect. How many employees read the Rules of Conduct for their positions that they are presented on entry? They are generally far too busy congratulating themselves on a new position and looking forward to their first paycheck.

Some civil servants have the responsibility of representing their country: through positions in immigration and customs in particular and through working for the security agency, the TSA, in the United States. Their actions can colour an individual's view of a whole nation. They don't realize that and the nation suffers as a result. In the author's experience, for example, Canada lacks both couth and intelligence.

A lesson to be learned from what we have seen is that a member of the public should take nothing lying down. The civil servant or company representative with whom you are dealing is probably neither the most senior civil servant in their department nor the CEO of their company. Their safe position depends on not making waves. Thus, one way to handle their poor behaviour is to threaten their day with a virtual tidal wave. This is best accomplished by going over their heads to their superior who, whatever happens, thereby sees that his employee cannot handle her or his job. If this isn't possible, another method is to reveal their actions or lack of action to the outside world by involving or threatening to involve outsiders. An Ombudsman is a first good step. Civil servants do not want anyone looking over their shoulder. Ombudsmen have a way of taking notes.

A second option is the press. The press love names (since everyone named will probably buy a copy of the newspaper) so it is very easy to tell a government employee or company representative that, without an immediate solution, the matter will be written up for the press, individually naming those responsible for the delay, the mis-justice, the lack of action and/or the lack of understanding. This strategy usually works wonders.

A third option is legal action but it usually goes no further than the threat.

It is hoped that this book will also give civil, Government, and company servants cause to consider the way they do their job. It doesn't take much to do one's job with understanding. Widen the slit of responses.

John Graham

Bibliography

"**Dr. Zhivago**," Boris Pasternak, first published 1957, Pantheon Books, New York, 1991, pp. 160-180

"**Animal Farm,**" George Orwell, Signet Books, London, 1945

"**Little Man, What now?**" Hans Fallada, Melville House Publishing, Brooklyn, NY, 2009, first published, "Kleiner Mann - was nun?" Rowohlt publishing, Berlin, 1932

"**The Tax Inspector,**" Peter Carey, Vintage, 1991

"**The Incredible Voyage – a Personal Odyssey**," Tristan Jones, Sheridan House, 1996

"**Snapshots of the Mind,**" John Graham, Publish America, Baltimore, Maryland, 2005

"**Codes of Conduct for Public Servants in Eastern and Central European Countries: A Comparative Perspective,**" Jolanta Palidauskaite, Ph.D., Department of Public Administration, Faculty of Social Sciences, Kaunas University of Technology, Lithuania, 2008

"**The Quiet Girl,**" Peter Hoeg, Audio Books, 2008

"**The Time Traveler's Guide to Medieval England, a Handbook for Visitors to the Fourteenth Century,**" Ian Mortimer, Simon and Schuster, New York, 2010

"**The History of the Medieval World,**" Susan Wise Bauer, W.W. Norton, New York, 2010

John Graham

"Last Call ... the rise and fall of prohibition,"
Daniel Okrent, Scribner, 2011

"The Information; a history, a theory, a flood," James
Gleick, Pantheon Books, New York, 2011

We are here to help you

Notes:

Date	Issue	Contact	Phone and e-mail	Response

John Graham

We are here to help you

John Graham